The
COMPANIONS *in Christ*

Network

www.companionsinchrist.org

So much more!

Companions in Christ offers *so much more* than printed resources. It offers an ongoing LEADERSHIP NETWORK that provides:

- ➤ Opportunities to connect with other churches who are also journeying through the *Companions in Christ* series.
- ➤ Helpful leadership tips and articles as well as updated lists of supplemental resources
- ➤ Training opportunities that develop and deepen the leadership skills used in formational groups
- ➤ An online discussion room where you can share or gather information
- ➤ Insights and testimonies from other *Companions in Christ* leaders
- ➤ FREE *Companions in Christ* posters to use as you promote the group in your congregation

Just complete this form and drop it in the mail, and you can enjoy the many bene-fits available through the Companions in Christ NETWORK! Or, enter your contact information at www.companionsinchrist.org/leaders.

- ☐ Add my name to the *Companions in Christ* NETWORK email list so that I can receive ongoing information about small-group resources and leadership trainings
- ☐ Please send me FREE *Companions in Christ* posters. Indicate quantity needed: (Also available online.)

Name: _____

Address: _____

City/State/Zip: _____

Church: _____

Email: _____

Phone: _____

COMPANIONS *in Chr*

Upper Room Ministries
PO Box 340012
Nashville, TN 37203-9540

D1410028

COMPANIONS *in Christ*

A SMALL-GROUP EXPERIENCE IN SPIRITUAL FORMATION

EXPLORING SPIRITUAL ~GUIDANCE

Participant's Book | Volume 5

Wendy M. Wright

UPPER ROOM BOOKS®

NASHVILLE

COMPANIONS IN CHRIST
EXPLORING SPIRITUAL GUIDANCE: THE SPIRIT OF CHRIST
Participant's Book: Part 5
Copyright © 2006 by Upper Room Books®
All rights reserved.

The Upper Room® Web site http://www.upperroom.org

At the time of publication all Web sites referenced in this book were valid. However, due to the fluid nature of the Internet some addresses may have changed or the content may no longer be relevant.

Unless otherwise stated, scripture quotations are from the New Revised Standard Version Bible, copyright © 1989 by the Division of Christian Education of the National Council of the Churches of Christ in the U.S.A. Used by permission. All rights reserved.

Scripture quotations designated REB are from *The Revised English Bible* (a revision of The New English Bible) and © Oxford University Press and Cambridge University Press 1989. Reprinted with permission.

Scripture quotations designated KJV are from The King James Version of the Bible.

Excerpts from *Christian Spiritual Formation in the Church and Classroom* by Susanne Johnson. Copyright © 1989 by Abingdon Press. Used by permission.

Excerpts from *Covenant Discipleship: Christian Formation through Mutual Accountability* by David Lowes Watson (Nashville, Tenn.: Discipleship Resources, 1991). Used by permission of the author.

Diagram from *The Spiritual Director: A Practical Guide*. Franciscan Herald Press, 1976. Used by permission of Franciscan Press.

Cover design: Left Coast Design, Portland, OR
Cover photo: Greg Scott; Masterfile
Interior icon development: Michael C. McGuire, settingPace
First printing: 2006

ISBN 0-8358-9834-2

Printed in the United States of America

**For more information on *Companions in Christ*
call 800-972-0433 or visit www.companionsinchrist.org**

Contents

Acknowledgments

Companions in Christ is truly the result of the efforts of a team of persons who shared a common vision. This team graciously contributed their knowledge and experience to develop a small-group resource that would creatively engage persons in a journey of spiritual growth and discovery. The author of Part 5 was Wendy M. Wright. Stephen Bryant was the primary author of the daily exercises and the Leader's Guide. Marjorie Thompson created the original design and participated in the editing of the entire resource. Keith Beasley-Topliffe served as a consultant in the creation of the process for the small-group meetings and contributed numerous ideas that influenced the final shape of the resource. In the early stages of development, two advisory groups read and responded to the initial drafts of material. The persons participating as members of those advisory groups were Jeannette Bakke, Avery Brooke, Thomas Parker, Helen Pearson Smith, Luther E. Smith Jr., Eradio Valverde Jr., Diane Luton Blum, Carol Bumbalough, Ruth Torri, and Mark Wilson. Prior to publication, test groups in the following churches used the material and provided helpful suggestions for improvement of the Participant's Books and the Leader's Guide.

First United Methodist Church, Hartselle, Alabama
St. George's Episcopal Church, Nashville, Tennessee

Acknowledgments

Northwest Presbyterian Church, Atlanta, Georgia
Garfield Memorial United Methodist Church,
    Pepper Pike, Ohio
First United Methodist Church, Corpus Christi, Texas
Malibu United Methodist Church, Malibu, California
First United Methodist Church, Santa Monica, California
St. Paul United Methodist Church, San Antonio, Texas
Trinity Presbyterian Church, Arvada, Colorado
First United Methodist Church, Franklin, Tennessee
La Trinidad United Methodist Church, San Antonio, Texas
Aldersgate United Methodist Church, Slidell, Louisiana

My deep gratitude goes to all these persons and groups for their contribution to and support of *Companions in Christ*.

—Janice T. Grana, editor of *Companions in Christ*
April 2001

Introduction

Welcome to Part 5 of *Companions in Christ*, a small-group resource for spiritual formation. This resource is designed to create a setting where you can respond to God's call to an ever-deepening communion and wholeness in Christ—as an individual, as a member of a small group, and as part of a congregation. The resource focuses on your experience of God and your discovery of spiritual practices that help you share more fully in the life of Christ. You will be exploring the potential of Christian community as an environment of grace and mutual guidance through the Spirit. You will grow closer to members of your small group as you seek together to know and respond to God's will. And your congregation will grow when you and your companions begin to bring what you learn into all areas of church life, from classes and meetings to worship and outreach.

How does *Companions in Christ* help you grow spiritually? It enables you to immerse yourself in "streams of living waters" through the spiritual disciplines of prayer, scripture, ministry, worship, study, and Christian conversation. These means of grace are the common ways in which Christ meets people, renews their faith, and deepens their life together in love. In the first four parts of *Companions in Christ*, you were introduced to the concept of spiritual formation as a journey, you explored the depths of scripture, you experienced new dimensions of prayer, and you reflected on Christ's call in your life.

In this fifth part, you and members of your group will grow together as a Christian community and gain skills in learning how small groups in the church become settings for spiritual guidance.

Although *Companions* is not an introductory course in Christianity for new Christians, it will help church people take up the basic disciplines of faith in renewing and transforming ways.

An Outline of the Resource

Companions in Christ has two primary components: individual reading and daily exercises throughout the week with this Participant's Book and a weekly two-hour meeting based on suggestions in the Leader's Guide. For each week, the Participant's Book has a chapter introducing new material and five daily exercises to help you reflect on your life in light of the content of the chapter. After the Preparatory Meeting of your group, you will begin a weekly cycle as follows: On day 1 you will be asked to read the chapter and on days 2–6 to complete the five daily exercises (found at the end of the chapter reading). On day 7 you will meet with your group. The daily exercises aim to help you move from information (knowledge about) to experience (knowledge of). An important part of this process is keeping a personal notebook or journal where you record reflections, prayers, and questions for later review and for reference at the weekly group meeting. The time commitment for the daily exercises is about thirty minutes. The weekly meeting will include time for reflecting on the exercises of the past week, for moving deeper into learnings from chapter readings, for having group experiences of prayer, and for considering ways to share with the congregation what you have learned or experienced.

The complete material in *Companions in Christ* covers a period of twenty-eight weeks divided into five parts or units, of which this volume is the fifth. The five parts are as follows:

1. *Embracing the Journey: The Way of Christ* (five weeks)—a basic exploration of spiritual formation as a journey toward wholeness and holiness, individually and in community, through the grace of God.

2. *Feeding on the Word: The Mind of Christ* (five weeks)—an introduction to several ways of meditating on and praying with scripture.

3. *Deepening Our Prayer: The Heart of Christ* (six weeks)—a guided experience of various forms and styles of prayer.

4. *Responding to Our Call: The Work of Christ* (five weeks)—a presentation of vocation or call: giving ourselves to God in willing obedience and receiving the fruits and gifts of the Holy Spirit.

5. *Exploring Spiritual Guidance: The Spirit of Christ* (five weeks)—an overview of different ways of giving and receiving spiritual guidance, from one-on-one relationships, to spiritual growth groups, to guidance in congregational life as a whole.

Your group may want to take a short break between units either to allow for some unstructured reflection time or to avoid meeting near Christmas or Easter. However, the units are designed to be sequential—each unit builds on previous ones.

This Participant's Book includes a section titled "Materials for Group Meetings." This section includes some brief supplemental readings that you will use as a part of one or more group meetings. Your leader will alert you when you will be using this material. Also you will find an annotated resource list that describes additional books related to the theme of this part of *Companions in Christ*.

You will need to bring your Participant's Book, your Bible, and your personal notebook or journal to the weekly group meeting.

The Companions in Christ Network

An additional dimension of *Companions in Christ* is the Network. While you and your group are experiencing *Companions in Christ*, groups in other congregations will also be meeting. The Network provides opportunities for you to share your experiences with one another and to link in a variety of meaningful ways. As you move through the resource, there will be occasions when you will be invited to pray for another group, send greetings or encouragement, or receive their support for your group. Connecting in these ways will enrich your group's experience and the experience of those to whom you reach out.

The Network also provides a place to share conversation and information. The Companion's Web site, www.companionsinchrist.org, includes a discussion room where you can offer insights, voice questions, and respond to others in an ongoing process of shared learning. The site provides a list of other Companions groups and their geographical locations so that you can make connections as you feel led.

The Companions Network is a versatile and dynamic component of the larger *Companions* resource. A Network toll-free number (1-800-972-0433) is staffed during regular business hours to take your order.

Your Personal Notebook or Journal

"I began these pages for myself, in order to think out my own particular pattern of living. . . . And since I think best with a pencil in my hand, I started naturally to write." Anne Morrow Lindbergh began her beloved classic, *Gift from the Sea*, with these words. You may not imagine that you "think best with a pencil in hand," but there is something truly wonderful about what can happen when we reflect on the inner life through writing.

Keeping a journal or personal notebook (commonly called journaling) will be one of the most important dimensions of your personal experience with *Companions in Christ*. The Participant's Book gives you daily spiritual exercises every week. More often than not, you will be asked to note your thoughts, reflections, questions, feelings, or prayers in relation to the exercises.

Even if you are totally inexperienced in this kind of personal writing, you may find that it becomes second nature very quickly. Your thoughts may start to pour out of you, giving expression to an inner life that has never been released. If, on the other hand, you find the writing difficult or cumbersome, give yourself permission to try it in a new way. Because a journal is "for your eyes only," you may choose any style that suits you. You need not worry about making your words sound beautiful or about writing with good grammar and spelling. You don't even need to write complete sentences! Jotting down key ideas, insights, or musings is just fine. You might want to doodle while you think or sketch an image that comes to you. Make journaling fun and relaxed. No one will see what you write, and you have complete freedom to share with the group only what you choose of your reflections.

There are two important reasons for keeping a journal or personal notebook as you move through *Companions in Christ*. First, the process of writing down our thoughts clarifies them for us. They become more specific and concrete. Sometimes we really do not know what we think until we see our thoughts on paper, and often the process of writing itself generates new creative insight. Second, this personal record captures what we have been experiencing inwardly over time. Journaling helps us track changes in our thinking and growth of insight. Our memories are notoriously fragile and fleeting in this regard. Specific feelings or creative connections we may have had two weeks ago, or even three days ago, are hard to recall without a written record. Even though your journal cannot capture all that goes through your mind in a single reflection period, it will serve as a reminder. You will need to draw on these reminders during small-group meetings each week.

Begin by purchasing a book that you can use for this purpose. It can be as simple as a spiral-bound notebook or as fancy as a cloth-bound blank book. Some people prefer lined paper and some unlined. You will want, at minimum, something more permanent than a ring-binder or paper pad. The Upper Room has made available a companion journal for this resource that you can purchase if you so desire. Or you can use the blank pages at the back of this book.

When you begin the daily exercises, have your journal and pen or pencil at hand. You need not wait until you have finished reading and thinking an exercise through completely. Learn to stop and write as you go. Think on paper. Feel free to write anything that comes to you, even if it seems to be "off the topic." It may turn out to be more relevant or useful than you first think. If the process seems clumsy at first, don't fret. Like any spiritual practice, it gets easier over time, and its value becomes more apparent.

Here is how your weekly practice of journaling is shaped. On the first day after your group meeting, read the new chapter. Jot down your responses to the reading: "aha" moments, questions, points of disagreement, images, or any other reflections you wish to record. You may prefer to note these in the margins of the chapter. Over the next five days, you will do the exercises for the week, recording either general or specific responses as they are invited. On the day of the group meeting, it will be helpful to review what you have written through the week, perhaps marking portions you would like to share in the group. Bring your journal with you to meetings so that you can refer to it directly or refresh your memory of significant moments you want to paraphrase during discussion times. With time, you may indeed find that journaling helps you to think out your own pattern of living and that you will be able to see more clearly how God is at work in your life.

Your Group Meeting

The weekly group meeting is divided into four segments. First you will gather for a brief time of worship and prayer. This offers an opportunity to set aside the many concerns of the day and center on God's presence and guidance as you begin your group session.

The second section of the meeting is called "Sharing Insights." During this time you will be invited to talk about your experiences with the daily exercises. The group leader will participate as a member and share his or her responses as well. Generally the sharing by each member will be brief and related to specific exercises. This is an important time for your group to learn and practice what it means to be a community of persons seeking to listen to God and to live more faithfully as disciples of Christ. The group provides a supportive space to explore your listening, your spiritual practices, and how you are attempting to put those practices into daily life. Group members need not comment or offer advice to one another. Rather the group members help you, by their attentiveness and prayer, to pay attention to what has been happening in your particular response to the daily exercises. The group is not functioning as a traditional support group that offers suggestions or help to one another. Rather, the group members trust that the Holy Spirit is the guide and that they are called to help one another listen to that guidance.

The "Sharing Insights" time presents a unique opportunity to learn how God works differently in each of our lives. Our journeys, while varied, are enriched by others' experiences. We can hold one another in prayer, and we can honor each other's experience. Through this part of the meeting, you will see in fresh ways how God's activity may touch or address our lives in unexpected ways. The group will need to establish some ground rules to facilitate the sharing. For example, you may want to be clear that each person speak only about his or her own beliefs, feelings, and responses and that all group members have permission to share only what and when they are ready to share. Above all, the group needs to maintain confidentiality so that what is shared in the group stays in the group. This part of the group meeting will be much less meaningful if persons interrupt and try to comment on what is being said or try to "fix" what they see as a problem. The leader will close this part of the meeting by calling attention to any patterns or themes that seem to emerge from the group's sharing. These patterns may point to a word that God is offering to the group. Notice that the group leader functions both as a participant and as someone who aids the process by listening and summarizing the key insights that have surfaced.

The third segment of the group meeting is called "Deeper Explorations." This part of the meeting may expand on ideas contained in the week's chapter, offer practice in the spiritual disciplines introduced in the chapter or exercises, or give group members a chance to reflect on the implications of what they are learning for themselves and for their church. It offers a common learning experience for the group and a chance to go deeper in our understanding of how we can share more fully in the mind, heart, and work of Jesus Christ.

As it began, the group meeting ends with a brief time of worship, an ideal time for the group to share special requests for intercession that might come from the conversation and experience of the meeting or other prayer requests that arise naturally from the group.

The weeks that you participate in *Companions in Christ* will offer you the opportunity to focus on your relationship with Christ and to grow in your openness to God's presence and guidance. The unique aspect of this experience is that members of your small group, who are indeed your companions on the journey, will encourage your searching and learning. Those of us who have written and edited this resource offer our prayers that God will speak to you during these weeks and awaken you to enlarged possibilities of love and service in Christ's name. As we listen and explore together, we will surely meet our loving God who waits eagerly to guide us toward deeper maturity in Christ by the gracious working of the Holy Spirit.

Exploring Spiritual Guidance: The Spirit of Christ

Wendy M. Wright

How Do I Know God's Will for My Life?

*I*n Part 4 we explored what it means to hear and respond to God's call in our lives. We looked at the importance of relying on God and recognizing our gifts as we seek to live faithful lives. But a growing clarity about vocation or call still does not make it easy to follow Christ. Every day we face decisions, opportunities, and challenges in the living out of our discipleship.

While still in graduate school, I was asked to give a retreat to a group of women on the theme "Women of Wisdom." In the arrogance of my youth and inexperience, I tended to see myself as the leader, come to share my learning with women who, because of their backgrounds, knew little about the historic spiritual wisdom of the Christian tradition. But during the course of this retreat, a woman approached me who turned out to be my teacher more than I hers. "For years I've been asking people wherever I go, how do I know God's will for my life?" she said excitedly. "No one ever gave me a good answer until recently, and I want to share that answer with you." I found myself intrigued because her question was not only a crucial one in the history of Christian spirituality but also a common and troubling question for many people today. What does God want of me? How do I live the Christian life? What is God's word to me in the various decisions I must make? Have I chosen the path God intends for me? In short, how do I know the will of God?

While call requires response and obedience, we will not be given a road map. . . . We are given building blocks to see what can be done with them, using for the task all of our intelligence, creativity, sensitivity, and love.

—Farnham, Gill, McLean, and Ward

My retreatant leaned closer to me and smiled. "If you think you can see God's will laid out neatly before you for the next five, ten, or twenty years as a clearly defined path, this is emphatically not the will of God. But if you sense that the next hesitant step you are about to make into an uncertain future is somehow directed by God, that is most probably God's will for you."

This woman's words have stuck with me over the years, both because she surprised me into listening for wisdom in unexpected places and because there is deep understanding in the words she passed on. Living into the Christian life in a serious and personal way is not an easy business. It is not a matter of simply following the rules or doing what we should. Sometimes it is a murky undertaking. It forces our childhood faith to change and grow. Life becomes more complex than we had planned. We may find ourselves at an impasse we never could have imagined. And while the living word of the gospel offers guidance, we discover that its application to our daily lives is not always clear. How do we "walk in God's ways"?

Discerning God's Will

A commonly held idea we need to abandon is that the "will of God" is some rigid, predetermined scheme we are expected to figure out, as if God had a great computerized master plan. In this view, our task (or rather our test) is to figure out how to "download" the plan and mechanically follow its instructions. A more helpful understanding of God's will might be described as "God's longing for our lives" or "the direction in which Love draws us." This divine longing is not merely private, although it is deeply personal. Love is drawing all of us. We respond to Love communally, as well as individually. Our response comes in the midst of family, work, our faith communities, and our larger communities. Perhaps it helps most to think about our response to God's will as our yes to the spirit of God that moves and lives among us, prompting, enlivening, and drawing us more deeply into the loving reality that God intends the world to be.

It would be naive to imagine that any of us could respond unfail-

When people seek God's will, their quest leads them to yearn for the will of God, even as God, in love, yearns for them.

Danny E. Morris and
Charles M. Olsen

ingly to the Spirit's promptings. Indeed, from the time of the early church, Christians have been aware that our ability to respond faithfully to God is compromised in countless ways. Sometimes we are so self-preoccupied, fearful, or swayed by other voices that we cannot even sense God's call to us. Our minds and hearts are full of confusing and conflicting messages, from both within and around us.

Perhaps if we look back to our adolescence, we can see this complex reality with stark clarity. In our teen years, the questions "Who am I?" and "What am I to do?" tended to be paramount. The culture said one thing and the church another; our parents and our peer groups pulled us in different directions; our childhood selves and our emerging adult selves likely added confusion. After making it through the struggles of adolescent identity, we probably discovered that our sense of identity continues to evolve. Indeed, God invites us throughout our lives to unlearn and relearn our most fundamental identity.

The Christian spiritual tradition refers to the process of sorting out the "voice" of God's spirit from other conflicting voices as the art of "discernment." Both tradition and experience confirm that discernment is truly a spiritual challenge.

For this reason, discernment is not typically a solitary practice in the church. Responding authentically to God's spirit happens best within the context of community, with the guidance of scripture, tradition, and other believers—all of which are means of grace. Discernment requires particular attention. We need to guide one another in discernment. Such guidance can take a number of forms that we will explore the next few weeks. For example, discernment can be practiced between two people in a form traditionally called spiritual direction. It is not direction in the usual meaning of that word. Rather, two people listen to understand and respond to the leading (the direction) of the Holy Spirit. Sometimes discernment has been practiced in small intentional communities such as faith-sharing or covenant groups. It has been the specific focus of certain practices such as the Quaker Clearness Committee, a small-group practice in which an individual or couple may gain clarity about a major concern or decision. Occasionally, the principles of discernment have been analyzed

Discernment often depends on gifts that we do not have. We need one another's insights, resources, and prayer.

—Jeannette A. Bakke

and a clear process outlined. Ignatius of Loyola did this in the sixteenth century with his *Spiritual Exercises*, an intense and structured program of guided prayer designed to realign the heart, mind, and will of the participant with the spirit of Christ.

Throughout its history, the church has been concerned about following the guidance of the Spirit and has affirmed that Christians can aid one another in this guidance. We all need the leading of the Spirit, so it may help us to consider the many ways we can open ourselves to this guidance within the community of Christ's disciples. Before enumerating these, however, it is important to distinguish spiritual guidance from other forms of guidance common to our experience.

Understanding Spiritual Guidance

First of all, spiritual guidance is not primarily about problem solving or about finding definitive answers to questions. It is more about living gratefully and gracefully into the rich, beautiful, painful texture of life and finding God there; more about sensing God's life-giving invitations in the midst of stagnation; more about living into the unfolding mystery of life of which we are a part. Thus spiritual guidance is not primarily counseling or therapy, although they are related fields. Spiritual guidance is not theological instruction or the giving of advice. Nor is it simply the friendly, commiserating listening that one neighbor might give to another. When we seek the guidance of the Spirit, we focus on the dynamic, living presence of God's spirit working in the life of an individual or community. Spiritual guidance can never simply apply generic principles to particular situations. It requires informed attention to the often surprising movement of God's spirit in concrete circumstances.

Why might you choose to seek out spiritual guidance, either as an individual or as a member of a group? Perhaps because you are haunted by the same unrelenting question that haunted my retreatant years ago: How do I know God's will for my life? Perhaps because even though your life is full of many things, it is somehow still empty, and God is the only "more" that can fill the gaping hole. Maybe the God you always thought you could count on has "disappeared" in the midst of death, divorce, or illness. Maybe you suddenly find yourself on fire with a new vision of the world, compelled to offer yourself generously in service. Or perhaps going to church once a week, and even to Bible study, is not meeting the urgent hunger you feel for prayer, the hunger to become more intimate with God.

Spiritual guidance is concerned with a person's entire life lived in response to God's leading, not only with the inner devotional world. Still it is not meant to take the place of other necessary forms of guidance offered within the faith community. A Twelve Step or similar program is essential for someone struggling with addiction. Marital difficulties, depression, career planning, or questions about what the church teaches are appropriately guided by trained counselors, therapists, and Christian educators. So spiritual guidance may help a person suffering from addiction, relational problems, work issues, or theological questions; but such guidance should not be expected to solve these issues. Rather, spiritual guidance assists a person in discovering the presence and guidance of God's spirit in the midst of all life's experiences.

Learning to Be Attentive

To be authentic and helpful in leading others toward knowledge of God's will, spiritual guidance needs to be carried out in a manner that differs somewhat from other helping professions. Attentiveness to God's spirit requires deeply receptive, prayerful listening. Practicing the art of attending to the Spirit involves us in contemplative listening. Such listening is quite distinct from the various ways in which we generally listen to one another. Think about it. In our common experience, we usually listen in self-referential ways. At a social gathering, we may appear to be listening to a guest but are really focused on what we will say in response to make an impression or keep the conversation going. We may listen primarily to form judgments, since we are often tempted to categorize people and events according to

We define Christian spiritual direction, then, as help given by one Christian to another which enables that person to pay attention to God's personal communication to him or her, to respond to this personally communicating God, to grow in intimacy with this God, and to live out the consequences of the relationship.

—William A. Barry and
William J. Connolly

Focused stillness creates an empty space in which to test the rough edges of experience and to discover wider perspectives. . . . Without cultivating times of silence and solitude, we cannot create an environment of obedient listening in which to hearken to God's voice.

—Thomas R. Hawkins

our norms of acceptability. We may listen for information, as we do in a classroom. Sometimes we listen carefully to another's argument in order to respond effectively to the argument. We may listen in order to sympathize and relieve someone's discomfort or to help solve the person's difficulties.

The kind of listening involved in spiritual guidance differs from these common ways of listening to one another. It is holy listening, rooted in silence. It seeks emptiness in order to be filled with the Spirit. It is permeated by humility. Such listening assumes that the Spirit is active among us and works through us. So it makes space for that movement. It is primarily receptive, patient, watchful, and waiting. Yet it does not fear action when action is called for. Such listening is generously flexible, hospitable, and warm. It embraces the widest possible spectrum of life's beauty and pain. It acknowledges the creation of all people in the image and likeness of God. It approaches life as a mystery into which we joyously and generously live. While in one sense a gift, such listening is generally cultivated over the years as we prayerfully attend to the Spirit in our own lives and as others listen to us in the same grace-filled way.

The focus in spiritual guidance is on a person's relationship with God and the responses that relationship calls forth. Since we are whole people and cannot separate our inner and outer lives, conversations in spiritual guidance may range over many topics—our families of origin, our ethnic or cultural roots, troubles with a spouse or children, the meaning of our work, the moral stands we take, the way we allocate our resources, the manner in which we schedule our time, the content and methods of our prayer, the spiritual disciplines we undertake, or the devotional exercises in which we engage. Any facet of life may come into consideration. But in spiritual guidance it will be considered in relation to the discerned movement of the Spirit. "How is God connected to this matter?" Here lies the root issue of spiritual guidance. When we pay attention in an open and discerning way, the God-connection in every aspect of our lives can become clear.

The following excerpt helps us understand what happens in a spiritual guidance relationship:

Spiritual direction is basically the guidance one Christian offers another to help that person "grow up in every way . . . into Christ (Eph. 4:15)." A spiritual guide is someone who can help us see and name our own experience of God. . . .

1. *A spiritual guide listens to us.* When we need someone to hear our life story in terms of faith, a spiritual guide offers hospitable space for us to speak and be heard. Often we do not fully know our thoughts or experiences, our questions or unresolved issues. We do not know until we have had a chance to put them into words before an attentive and receptive ear. A spiritual director can "listen us into clarity," helping us articulate our thoughts, feelings, questions, and experiences in relation to God.

2. *A spiritual guide helps us to notice things.* God's presence and the ways of the Spirit are not generally self-evident to us. They are subtle and unobtrusive, often hidden in the midst of ordinary events and interactions. It takes practice to see the grace of God in everyday life. A spiritual mentor can help us pay attention to signs of grace, to listen for "God's still small voice" in our daily encounters and experiences. A guide can also direct our attention to the dynamics of our heart, so that we can become more aware of how God speaks to us through it.

3. *A spiritual guide helps us to respond to God with greater freedom.* When we begin to notice God's presence, guidance, provision, and challenge in our daily lives, we are faced with choices. How shall we respond? The choice is not always easy. God's presence and provision are comforting, naturally eliciting gratitude and praise. But God also faces us with the darker realities in our lives, calling us to genuine change. It is hard to let go of old habits and ways of being. Out of this encounter, God calls us to a new sense of purpose and mission in life. A spiritual director can encourage us toward a fuller freedom to respond to God in loving obedience.

4. *A spiritual guide points us to practical disciplines of spiritual growth.* Without the help of particular practices it is difficult to become more aware of, and responsive to, God's activity in our lives. Most of us could use guidance on ways of prayer that attune us to God's presence. We may need suggestions for spiritual reading, tips on keeping a journal, or reminders about the nature of authentic humility in self-examination. Perhaps we need someone who has practiced fasting to help us stay on track with our efforts. A spiritual companion can suggest various practices to us as they seem

appropriate and help us to discern when and whether to change them. A guide can also help keep us accountable for the disciplines we commit ourselves to.

5. *A spiritual guide will love us and pray for us.* This is probably the most important function of a companion in Christian faith. The love of a spiritual director for the one directed is always mediated by the love of Christ. It is agape love. The ongoing expression of that love is faithful prayer, both within and beyond meeting times. If this is in effect, many inadequacies in a guide can be covered by grace. If it is not present, even virtuoso technique can scarcely make up for it! [1]

DAILY EXERCISES

Margaret Guenther writes the following:

> So what does the spiritual director teach? In the simplest and also most profound terms, the spiritual director is simultaneously a learner and a teacher of discernment. What is happening? Where is God in this person's life? What is the story? Where does this person's story fit in our common Christian story?[2]

This week's daily exercises invite us to explore the gift of holy listening to God's presence in one another's lives. Use your time to reflect with the exercises and to commune with God in prayer.

EXERCISE 1

Read 1 Samuel 3:1-18 with an eye toward Eli's role as a spiritual guide with Samuel. How did Eli respond to Samuel, and what did Eli do that helped Samuel recognize God's call in his experience? How would you have responded to Samuel's persistence? Identify the "Elis" in your life who have listened to you with patience and helped you name your experience of God.

Review the five points of what happens in a spiritual guidance relationship printed on pages 00-00. Reflect on where you see any of these dynamics at work in the story of Samuel or in your own relationships.

EXERCISE 2

Read Acts 8:26-40. The story of Philip with the Ethiopian eunuch reveals dimensions of evangelism and faith sharing but also of a spiritual guidance relationship. List the features of spiritual guidance that you see illustrated here. Have you had relationships that shared such features? What made those experiences good or difficult?

EXERCISE 3

Read Acts 8:26-40 again. Write a first-person account of the Ethiopian eunuch sharing with Philip some aspect of his search for wholeness. Pay close attention to clues the story gives about the man's situation:

where he is going, where he is coming from, and whether he finds what he was looking for (see Deut. 23:1). Use your imagination to identify with the eunuch. Why might he feel separated from his own creative vitality? What might draw him to the passage from Isaiah? Take a moment to reflect on where you can actually identify with the eunuch's situation in your current life.

EXERCISE 4

Read Acts 8:26-40 a third time. Write a first-person account of Philip's journey with the Ethiopian eunuch. Use your imagination to identify with Philip. Describe how your relationship with the eunuch unfolded. Explore how you received the Spirit's guidance even as you were offering guidance—from start to finish in this relationship.

In closing, bring to mind someone you will be seeing soon. Lift this person to God in prayer and, when you do meet, follow the lead of Christ's spirit. Later, record your experience and insights.

EXERCISE 5

A particularly helpful spiritual exercise in discerning God's movement in your life is called "the examen," a structured and regular review of daily life that emphasizes either assessment of your faithfulness (examination of conscience) or awareness of God's presence (examination of consciousness). In this final part of *Companions in Christ*, the last of each week's daily exercises is an invitation to various forms of daily examen. Typically, the examen is practiced on a daily basis, but we will be using it as a weekly exercise.

The following examen is adapted from Ben Campbell Johnson's process for "integrating the life of prayer into the ordinary events and decisions of everyday life." Keep your journal handy to make notes.

> *Gather the week.* Identify the ten or twelve major events of your week, including prayer, particular conversations, meetings, meals, work, and planned or unplanned occurrences. List them.
>
> *Review the week.* Reflect upon each occurrence listed. Recall what was happening within you, what you were feeling, and how you were reacting or responding. This is the actual substance of your daily life.

Give thanks for the week. Thank God for each part of your week, for your life, for the lives of others who were part of your week, and for God's presence in your week. Celebrate the particular gifts you received in the expected and unexpected occurrences that enriched your week.

Confess your sin. Acknowledge your faults in thought, word, and deed toward God, neighbor, creation, and yourself. Name the times when you feel you may have ignored subtle promptings or warnings of the Spirit.

Seek the meaning of the events. Reflect on the underlying significance of each event. Ask yourself such questions as, What is the theme of the week's events, gifts, and challenges? Where did Jesus experience something similar and how did he respond? What is God saying to me or inviting me to learn? What am I being called to do? Write down what comes to mind.[3]

Remember to review your journal entries for the week in preparation for the group meeting.

Part 5, Week 2
Spiritual Companions

*I*deally, the entire church should be a community of spiritual discernment. In a sense, that is what the church is meant to be—a community focused on discerning and doing the will of God. Unfortunately too few people experience the church this way. Church activities tend to focus on evangelism, church growth, fund-raising, teaching and learning groups, programs for children and youth, or crisis intervention for families and individuals in need. These are all significant and necessary functions. Yet they leave many people empty, departing from classrooms, fellowship halls, or sanctuaries with their spiritual hunger unmet. As Christians, we may draw on a rich heritage of well-tested models and promising experiments in spiritual guidance to feed that hunger.

The Gospel of Luke (24:13-35) tells a story that reveals something important to us about spiritual guidance. After the crucifixion, two disappointed and distraught disciples were walking down the road that led to Emmaus. They met a stranger with whom they shared news about the terrible events of the last few days. Inviting him to stay with them as the day drew to a close, the disciples recognized the stranger as Jesus when he broke bread with them. After his departure, the disciples could scarcely contain their excitement! "Didn't our hearts burn within us when he spoke to us on the road?" they asked.

Conversion [is] a lifelong process of letting God remove the scales from our eyes so that we can more and more embrace the reality of God's overwhelming love for us. In this lifelong process of withdrawal and return we need one another to help us to overcome our resistance to the light.

—William A. Barry

Six centuries after this Gospel story was written down, Gregory the Great commented on this passage. God, he said, is experienced among us in just the same way as on the road to Emmaus. God is known by the burning of our hearts, known in our shared love of God, known as existing between us. Indeed, God is known precisely when we journey with one another, talking of the questions dearest to our hearts and finding there both companionship and God's living presence.

The Christian spiritual life, although intimate and personal, can never be isolated or privatized if it is to remain authentic. We share this life together. From the earliest centuries, Christians have affirmed that spiritual discernment is best done with at least one, if not several other believers. From the past we get a glimpse into the variety of ways spiritual companionship has been practiced.

One-on-One Spiritual Guidance

Perhaps the most classic form of one-on-one spiritual companionship is found in the deserts of Egypt, Palestine, and Syria during the fourth through sixth centuries. The church had passed through a period of intense persecution when martyrdom had been the height of Christian witness. Now a different kind of martyrdom became a witness to new life in Christ. Many embraced the "white martyrdom" of the ascetic life (rather than the "red martyrdom" of physical death). Through practices of prayer, self-discipline, and mortification, the ascetic martyr "died" to his or her "false self"—the proud, greedy, grandiose self admired by the general culture—and was reborn to the "true self" in Christ—the charitable, humble, other-centered self of a pure heart. Such radical transformation was understood to be a real struggle with the "demons" that disfigure the human heart.

Those who sought this new life went to the deserts looking for spiritual mentors who had been through the forge of transformation and had emerged reborn. Charismatic figures, such as Anthony of Egypt, were legendary. They had authority because of their gift of discernment. They were gifted to see into the hearts of those who came to them and to perceive what particular demons had gripped them. Out of their own hard-won experience they could offer guidance in the process of opening one's heart to the transfiguring grace of God. In the silence and solitude of the desert, a deep capacity for listening could be cultivated, a listening for the word of God, a listening for the brush of the Spirit.[1]

The one-on-one mentoring relationship between a seeker and a spiritual abba (father) or amma (mother) was one of intense trust, obedience, and spiritual intimacy. The seeker unguardedly opened his or her heart before the elder, revealing all its thoughts and movements; and the elder could then discern what was needed. From that tradition we have collections of "Sayings" that give us a glimpse into the wisdom these masters passed on to their disciples. Here are two examples of writing from these collections:

> A brother asked one of the elders: What good thing shall I do, and have life thereby? The old man replied: God alone knows what is good. However, I have heard it said that someone inquired of Father Abbot Nisteros the great, the friend of Abbot Anthony, asking: What good work shall I do? And that he replied: Not all works are alike. For Scripture says that Abraham was hospitable and God was with him. Elias loved solitary prayer, and God was with him. And David was humble, and God was with him. Therefore, whatever you see your soul to desire according to God, do that thing, and you shall keep your heart safe.[2]

> Amma Syncletica said: It is good not to get angry. But if it should happen, do not allow your day to go by affected by it. For it is said: Do not let the sun go down. Otherwise, the rest of your life may be affected by it. Why hate a person who hurts you, for it is not that person who is injust, but the devil. Hate the sickness, but not the sick person.[3]

This early desert model of spiritual guidance has persisted over the centuries with some variations. Holy Christian men and women, authenticated by their gifts, the fruits of their works, and the holiness of their lives, have always gathered disciples around themselves. In the church of the Middle Ages many holy women, some of them visionaries or prophets, functioned as spiritual guides in their communities. In fourteenth-century England, a woman named Julian lived in a hermitlike cell in the city of Norwich and listened to the spiritual concerns of people in all walks of life who came to the window of her cell.

There is the clear call to perfection, to holiness, to fullness of life in Christ. The call to be perfect (teleios) (Phil. 3.15) is variously translated as a call to spiritual maturity (RSV and NEB) and to spiritual adulthood (J. B. Phillips). It is this process of spiritual maturing which is the purpose of spiritual direction.

—Kenneth Leech

Another holy woman of the same century named Catherine, from the Italian city of Siena, was called "mother" by her band of spiritual disciples. Her urgent, scolding letters to public figures, including the pope, were heeded because of her reputation as a trustworthy guide in discerning God's spirit.

This one-on-one model of guidance has historically taken other forms, some linked to other institutional roles within the church. In the Middle Ages, the practice of one-on-one spiritual direction became more a function of the clergy who often advised people in approved methods of prayer and formal principles of the spiritual life.

Today, one-on-one spiritual guidance has returned more to the early model. We can see clear examples of this in Jesus' gracious relationship to his band of disciples and in the caring companionship of the early church. Discernment is a gift given to the church for the good of the church, exercised by certain people regardless of whether they are men, women, laity, clergy, or officeholders in the church. The focus is on the individual's growing relationship with God. The spiritual director or guide facilitates the growth and development of that relationship. The individual's experience of God is the starting point and is always to be revered. Contemporary spiritual guides do not see themselves primarily as "answer people" or "fix-it people." They are not gurus or master teachers who tell others what to do. They do not foster dependence or assume inordinate importance in the lives of those they seek to guide. Rather, they are in the service of God and the person who comes to them.[4] A spiritual guide offers a safe, confidential space to look at one's life in the light of God's presence and purposes. Because the spiritual guidance relationship focuses entirely on the person and his or her relationship with God, the spiritual guide enables the seeker to name what is happening in life's struggles, surprises, and challenges. By going beneath the surface of life's events, the person seeking guidance can make connections with scripture and insights from spiritual tradition, listening and responding to God's call.

Howard Rice has written a simple description of the nature of one-on-one spiritual guidance:

In a one-on-one relationship, the spiritual guide's responsibilities are these:

1. to listen carefully to what people say about themselves and their spiritual lives,
2. to encourage their desire (expressed or hinted at) to recognize and respond to God's presence in their lives,
3. to suggest the practice of certain disciplines that will enable spiritual growth and open them to the Holy Spirit's presence,
4. to challenge them to examine their lives honestly in the light of God's forgiving love, and
5. to pray with and for them.[5]

Spiritual Friendship

A variation of one-on-one spiritual guidance is spiritual friendship. Spiritual direction and spiritual friendship are not equivalent. In a relationship between a spiritual guide and the person seeking guidance, there is a certain asymmetry. The focus is upon the relationship between God and the person seeking guidance, upon that person's life and prayer rather than the life of the guide. On occasion the spiritual guide's personal experience might explicitly enter in but only if it could be of help in some way to the individual seeker.

Spiritual friendship, on the other hand, is an utterly mutual and equal relationship. The sharing between two such friends goes both ways, eliciting mutual self-disclosure. Friends see themselves as peers. Neither sees the other as more experienced or authoritative. A healthy interdependency grows between them.

The church's history provides wonderful examples of spiritual friendships. The Celtic church honored the tradition of the "anmchara" or soul-friend, a wise companion who took it upon himself or herself to accompany another on the soul's journey. And history gives us insight into beautiful lives of faith sustained by friendship. Francis de Sales wrote of friendship as absolutely necessary for people intent on living more devoutly. He believed that a devout life "in the world" needed all the care and support it could get! Mutual commitment to a Christian life and care for each other's growth in that

[Our lives] will be enriched by the gift of a listening ear—one who will pay attention to movements of grace and the tremors of change. Listening for the whispers of God is one of the most prized gifts we can offer each other.

—Larry J. Peacock

life is the main content of spiritual friendship. At its root lies a shared desire for God.[6]

Today spiritual friendship takes many forms. We may discover a group of friends who support us in faith or a particular friend who journeys with us for a short period or over many years. Such friendships vary greatly, as individuals differ. They may arise spontaneously, but if they adopt an intentional structure, they can allow for that careful listening, encouragement, and admonition in which mutual self-disclosure occurs regularly and fruitfully.[7]

Communities of Spiritual Guidance

Christians have discerned the movement of the Spirit in intimate settings of one-on-one guidance throughout their history. But they have also created intentional communities to facilitate growth in the Spirit. The parish or congregation is meant to be such a community. We have noted that in our recent history, discernment has typically been lost in congregational life. Today, however, there is increasingly conscious reflection on the local church and the role of the pastor as spiritual guide, not only to individuals, but also to the congregation as a whole.[8] Considerable interest and attention have been given to the art of discernment as practiced by governing church boards.[9]

More typically, Christians have formed small intentional groupings to provide spiritual encouragement. Monasticism is one long-lived experiment in creating a permanent vessel of spiritual formation. The desert ideal of allowing God to transform the "false self" into the "true self" became institutionalized in the monastic life. The rule of life that governed the monastic community became a living word spoken to guide members of the monastery into the Spirit-transformed life. The rule not only provided an administrative structure for community life; it embodied the spiritual values the monastery sought to foster. For example, the Rule of Saint Benedict (the Western church's most famous monastic rule) allowed such values as silence, prayer, study, stability, and hospitality to be incorporated into the daily life of the monks.[10]

Spiritual guidance went on well beyond the walls of the monastery. There have been many other efforts to guide one another communally. The High Middle Ages saw the rise of the Christian laity. Sometimes women and men who raised families and worked "in the world" joined "third orders," associate groups sponsored by formal religious orders such as the Franciscans or Dominicans. These "third order" associates followed a daily rule modified to suit their obligations. They met regularly with their spiritual mentors for guidance.

Sometimes groups of laypersons or mixed groups of clergy and laity were established for spiritual nurture. One such movement, the Beguines, flourished in the thirteenth century. This movement was mainly for women who sometimes lived in their family homes and sometimes lived together. They shared prayer and good works and grew together into the Christian life. During later centuries in continental Europe, a spiritual movement known as the Modern Devotion arose. Out of it grew groups such as the Brothers and Sisters of the Common Life. These laypeople lived together in small groups, often sharing a similar occupation like textile work. They were part of an ordinary congregation but were more serious than most Christians about the spiritual life. They wrote and circulated devotional manuals, met to read scripture together, and held shared scripture reflections to which they invited guests. And they regularly examined their actions together in light of the gospel.

These same basic components of shared guidance could be found in the churches that grew out of the Protestant Reformation. Calvin encouraged spiritual growth in his congregations through individual care, correspondence, and informal mutual support. His spiritual heirs, the Puritans, were enthusiastic about public sharing of spiritual experience and were encouraged to choose peers to whom they could give account of the workings of God in the soul. The Puritans were great correspondents and journalers, often using their diaries as a way of practicing self-examination. Giving advice and sharing accounts of one's spiritual journey by letter were popular Puritan practices.

We find the most intentional and systematic Protestant effort to encourage spiritual guidance in the early Methodist movement. John

Wesley believed that Christians grow in holiness most effectively in mutually supportive group settings. He devised a system of guidance for every conceivable need within the Christian community. The United Societies were open to anyone and met weekly for prayer, mutual exhortation, and stewardship accountability. The class meetings, smaller units that met in homes under lay leadership, undertook to commit members to a more intentional spiritual discipline. Bands, separate-sex meetings of even smaller numbers, fostered mutual spiritual maturity in a peer setting. Select societies were for those who felt themselves called to the serious pursuit of holiness.[11]

Most churches of the Radical Reformation emphasized group spiritual guidance. The Moravians gathered in small groups for mutual admonition. And the Quakers (Society of Friends) cultivated a style of worship—the silent meeting—that was essentially the practice of corporate discernment. Listening in attentive silence for the Inner Light that could illumine the way of the community was its goal. The Quakers also developed other means of shared spiritual guidance. For example, the Clearness Committee gathered a company of selected listeners or questioners to help individuals clarify God's will in specific moments of decision making.

Today most spiritual guidance takes place with persons meeting face-to-face. However, letters, telephone calls, and even E-mail communication can provide opportunities for exchange among Christians hungry to grow in God. All these models share the common goals of growing in spiritual maturity, discerning God's living spirit, and developing an authentic relationship with God.

The Influence of Culture

One interesting question is the extent to which these various models of spiritual guidance are rooted exclusively in European thought forms and cultural practices. Clearly, Western Christianity has provided much of the spiritual wisdom known to us and still relevant to our churches today. That wisdom is wide and broad but needs further examination in our cross-cultural context. The task of examin-

A Christian community is essential for discernment. The community may be represented by one person who is part of the larger Christian community and brings its faith and values to a particular situation. Or several people may be a community that will focus on the needs of one person by his or her invitation. No one should attempt spiritual discernment by himself or herself without putting decisions to the test of other spiritual friends.

—Danny E. Morris and Charles M. Olsen

ing the influence of culture on spiritual guidance models is relatively new but important. The related question of gender differences has already received some attention. Many now affirm that women bring to spiritual guidance a unique perspective that their male counterparts do not generally share and that issues of power, violence, and anger often alter the way women relate to God.[12]

But the cultural question is still new. Differences in culture influence our image of God and shape our religious experience, which can profoundly affect the practice of spiritual formation. For example, Americans of European ancestry often stress the individual's relationship to the world and God. Persons from cultures outside North America may emphasize the community and the extended family and thus may experience the world and God in a different way. Faith sharing and spiritual formation in Central and Latin America reflect the context of political and economic oppression in that part of the world. Thus God's Word is not solely for personal consolation and salvation but is seen as socially and spiritually liberating for the poor and redeeming for entire classes of people.

Culturally determined patterns of communication also influence spiritual formation. For example, the religious practices of many African Americans are characterized by emotional expressiveness and a strong sense of group solidarity. The dominant one-on-one Western model of spiritual guidance that stresses silence, solitude, and introspection may not be helpful for Christians whose deepest religious experiences have been forged in other settings. Persons from Asian cultures, in which respect for and obedience to authority is deeply embedded, may find the egalitarian model of spiritual friendship unworkable, especially in relation to authority figures such as pastors or teachers. In the context of spiritual guidance, all of these questions need to be considered, not in ways that stereotype people, but in ways that respect the unique experience of each person.[13]

DAILY EXERCISES

Douglas Steere writes of a holy moment in 1950 in the midst of a Quaker meeting at Haverford College. Martin Buber, the renowned Jewish scholar and rabbi, was a guest at the college. He rose from the silence of a Quaker meeting to speak. "[Buber] told us that it was a great thing to transcend barriers and to meet another human being, but that *meeting* another across a barrier was not the greatest thing one man could do for another. There was still something greater. The greatest thing . . . was to *confirm* the deepest thing he has within him. After this, he sat down as abruptly as he had arisen. There was little more to say." [14]

This week's daily exercises invite us to explore how we see faithful friends and guides in scripture confirming for one another the deepest thing they have within them. How do we experience the same?

Exercise 1

Read 1 Samuel 18:1-4; 23:15-18. The stories of David and Jonathan illustrate the gift and joy of genuine friendship. Identify the qualities of spiritual friendship that you see here. Then describe any friendship you have known in your life that embodies such qualities. Who among your friends now helps you find strength in God? How does that happen? Give thanks to God for this person or these persons.

Exercise 2

Read 2 Samuel 11:26–12:13. Nathan demonstrates a prophetic dimension of spiritual guidance when he confronts David with the truth about himself. Do you currently struggle with whether to tell a friend or acquaintance a hard truth or to mind your own business? Look for guidance in Nathan's relationship with David and his manner of speaking the truth in love. Take your situation to God in prayer. Listen for whether the Lord is sending you in love to speak, to listen, to learn, or to confess and examine a hidden sin in your life.

EXERCISE 3

Read John 4:1-26. The story of Jesus and the Samaritan woman illustrates Jesus' capacity to see through layers of cultural identity to who persons are in God's "truth." Explore the way Jesus calls the woman to insight, constantly drawing her toward a deeper awareness of "the gift of God" (v. 10) in her midst. Look for when and how Jesus tries to move her beyond conventional or surface ways of seeing him, herself, and God. Notice where Jesus invites her to go from the theological to the personal realm, and how she responds to him.

What insights did this reading bring to you about the nature of spiritual guidance or friendship? Take a moment to be aware of the gift of God in you and to ask for the drink of living water that you need.

EXERCISE 4

Read John 4:1-42. The story of Jesus and the Samaritan woman illustrates communal as well as personal effects of spiritual guidance. The fact that the woman came to the well "about noon" gives us a clue to the possibility of her isolation from the community. Most village women would come to the well in the early morning or late afternoon, not in the heat of the day. This fact, coupled with the woman's marital history and current situation, might suggest a socially unaccepted existence among her own people—somewhat like the way in which Jews viewed Samaritans as unacceptable.

In light of her isolation and lack of acceptance by her community, explore the ripple effects of Jesus' actions as a spiritual guide toward this Samaritan woman. How does Jesus' spiritual guidance impact her relationship to the community? What is the potential impact on the relationship between this Samaritan community and the Jewish community? Record your insights.

EXERCISE 5

Use the model for examen of daily life provided last week (pages 244–45). Or try the one outlined here that reviews your life through the lens of the Lord's Prayer. Enter the process in prayer; ask God to assist you in remembering your life in truth and grace; record thoughts in your journal.

"Our Father in heaven, hallowed be your name"—*How have you attended to God's holy presence in your life this week? Where and in what ways were you especially aware or unaware of God?*

"Your kingdom come, your will be done, on earth as in heaven"—*In what ways did you seek God's will? In what ways did you succeed or fail in allowing God's yearning for the common good to rule your attitudes and actions?*

"Give us today our daily bread"—*What is the bread, physical and spiritual, that sustained you this week and for which you are grateful to God? What did you do with bread beyond your needs? With whom did you break bread or share your bread?*

"Forgive us our sins as we forgive those who sin against us"—*Did you forgive those who offended or harmed you? What steps remain to restore the peace? Whom did you harm, and what actions did you take to make amends? What steps remain?*

"Save us from the time of trial and deliver us from evil"—*Where was your faith (patience, love, hope) tested this week? In what ways did you fail the test? In what ways were you delivered? What did you learn about your limits and where to find the strength you need?*

"For the kingdom, the power, and the glory are yours, now and forever"—*Give thanks to God for divine blessing and bounty. Name the blessings of this past week and relinquish them to God. Spend time in prayer praising God and rededicating your life to walking with Christ.*

Review your journal entries for the week in preparation for the group meeting.

Part 5, Week 3
Small Groups for Spiritual Guidance

In fourteenth-century Italy, a remarkable woman named Catherine who lived in the town of Siena authored a book titled *The Dialogue*. It recorded an account of a conversation between God and "a soul." In it Catherine writes that God speaks of the church as a great vineyard in which each individual has his or her own vine garden but in which there are no fences or dividing lines between the gardens. Whatever happens in one's own vineyard, for good or for ill, intimately affects every other vineyard.

Clearly, Catherine of Siena was developing the biblical image of the vine and the branches of which Jesus speaks in John 15. But she did not understand the image in an individualistic way. Not only are we nurtured by a common source—Christ, the Vine—but we are interconnected and thus help nurture one another as well. The fruitfulness of the entire vineyard—the church—is shared by all of us, not only as recipients but as assistant gardeners. Our weeding, pruning, fertilizing, and planting are not only for ourselves; they are for all of us together. Scripture underscores this idea with other metaphors like the church as one body with many members but one Spirit (1 Cor. 12; Eph. 4). Our growth in God is a communal venture!

In a profound sense, whatever spiritual cultivation we do as individuals ultimately affects our families, our communities, and the entire world. This communal dimension is a natural and inevitable

At their best, [small prayer, faith, and discernment groups] provide an arena for corporate openness to the Spirit's way, personal support, the perspective of others' views, and opportunities for sharing pain, anxiety, thanksgiving, prayer for others, and surrender to God in faith.

—Tilden H. Edwards

consequence of the spiritual life. But some methods of spiritual cultivation in the Christian community explicitly recognize that spiritual nurture is a shared undertaking. Several forms of spiritual guidance are available for small groups to explore. Although the following will not exhaust the possibilities, we may distinguish among (1) mutual accountability groups, (2) scripture-focused groups, (3) prayer-focused groups, (4) action-reflection groups, and (5) group spiritual guidance.

While these small-group models are distinct, they share a common goal of helping us open ourselves more generously to the prompting of the Spirit. They may involve elements of study or information gathering, but the primary purpose of such groups is not to help us acquire more information; rather, it is to help change, mold, and shape us more closely to the divine image in which we are originally made. In our present information age that highly values quick access to facts and figures, it is sometimes hard to remember that the spiritual life does not follow this path. We do not acquire a new technique of prayer and expect it to earn the favor or presence of God for us. Instead, we become people of prayer. We do not purchase a how-to book and follow the simple instructions labeled "Five Secrets of the Successful Spiritual Person" or "Ten Guaranteed Traits for Gaining Spiritual Mastery." Spiritual formation more closely resembles a love relationship to which we commit, surrender, and open ourselves. Through this relationship we are challenged, taught, gifted, and loved unconditionally. And by it, we are changed.

The wonderful mystery of the church as a fruitful vineyard is that there are many others like us yearning and struggling to open themselves to the embrace of love. This is not something we do alone.

Mutual Accountability Groups

One way gathered Christians have opened themselves to God is through mutual accountability or covenant groups. The group members agree to practice specific disciplines of the Christian life individually, then meet to support and hold one another accountable.

One popular model is that of covenant discipleship groups. Wesleyan scholar David Lowes Watson has recovered this model from historical Methodist sources.[1] Based on the group practices of the early Wesleyan movement, Watson has shown contemporary Christians the core genius of the early Methodist class meetings. The underlying concept is that people go to God most readily with mutual support and encouragement. A small group of committed Christians (up to seven) agrees to journey together. They look to Wesley's understanding of the Christian life and see that acts of compassion, justice, devotion, and worship are all necessary for such a life. Group members consider specific ways they might carry out such acts: for example, visiting persons who are unable to leave their homes is an act of compassion, daily Bible reading is an act of devotion, advocating for prisoners of conscience is an act of justice, and attending Sunday services is an act of worship. The group members then create a written covenant to which they agree to hold one another accountable. Regular meetings are held in which members give account to one another for the ways they have lived out their shared covenant between meetings. Participants encourage, support, and advise one another. The underlying premise of this model is that practicing these central Christian disciplines is spiritually formative and that we grow together and individually as we practice acts of mercy and piety.

Emmaus groups and other expressions of the Cursillo tradition practice another model. These little discipleship groups of two to six persons meet weekly for an hour around a common format. Members review their awareness of Christ's presence and call to discipleship during the past week and how they responded. Then they share how they are doing with their spiritual disciplines in the area of prayer (personal and corporate), study (scripture and other spiritual reading), and service (in church and community). Finally, they name their plans for walking with Christ in the week to come, closing with prayers for one another and others. The group's purpose is to provide ongoing support and caring accountability for one another's commitment to live wholly in the grace of God and to grow in the self-giving spirit of Jesus Christ.

Another expression of the mutual accountability group is the Renovaré model developed by James Bryan Smith and established by Richard Foster.[2] This ecumenical process for small groups identifies five basic traditions of the Christian life: contemplative, holiness, charismatic, social justice, and evangelical. A small group of people (two to seven) gather to explore these five elements in an outlined set of meetings. The group considers what it might mean to discover (1) a life of intimacy with God, (2) a life of purity and virtue, (3) a life of empowerment through the Spirit, (4) a life of justice and compassion, and (5) a life founded upon the Word. Once formed, the group continues meeting to account for the way participants are living in relation to these traditions and so that group members can share their ongoing faith journeys with one another.

Other types of covenant groups may function differently. They may exist for a specific period of time and serve mainly as a small community in which faith stories can be shared. Generally, they will covenant to honor mutual openness, compassion, encouragement, and confidentiality. The element of mutual commitment to spiritual formation through a written covenant characterizes these groups.

Scripture-Focused Groups

In small groups, Christ's light shines more clearly. There is a holy mystery in groups as words are spoken that open windows to the soul in another and all sit in awe and wonder. Groups can be the arena for growth in the spiritual life.

—Larry J. Peacock

A second type of small group focuses on scripture. Most churches sponsor Bible study groups that have an important place in the life of any faith community. Often, the emphasis in such groups does not go beyond study. Their main purpose is to read and learn about scripture more intentionally. However, a formation group focused on scripture will emphasize shared reflection on the Word. Meditating on scripture is understood to reveal the leading of the Spirit in the lives of participants.[3] The ancient practice of *lectio divina* or meditative reading might guide such a group. You have had opportunities in earlier units to experience this practice through the daily exercises. As you know, the purpose of slow, reflective reading is to engage our whole selves with the text. We read first simply for content, considering perhaps the meaning of the text in its original communal setting. Then we allow ourselves to let the text—even one word or image from it—work on us. It settles in us, and we may begin to converse with God about it, turn it over in our hearts, feel it speaking to our lives. Such prayerful "chewing" of the Word often results in a deep, reverent resting in God, a contemplative embrace of the depth of the Word without much thinking or talking. A group that practices *lectio* may focus on each individual's reflections on the Word; or it may merge into shared *lectio*, a prayerful "reading" of scripture as it unfolds in the life of the group.

Prayer-Focused Groups

Still a third type of formation group centers on prayer. These groups vary according to the type of prayer emphasized. The most common form focuses on intercessory prayer, perhaps conscious that the "vineyard without fences" is not merely an encouraging or educational metaphor. We do indeed participate in others' lives at a deep level. The intentions of our prayers, offered on behalf of one another, shape and direct the intentions that circulate in our world. We are interconnected spiritual beings. Acting on the same principle, some prayer groups dedicate themselves specifically to praying for healing of one another and the world.

Also popular today are centering prayer groups, given form by Thomas Keating and others.[4] As you learned in the third unit on prayer, centering prayer is a practice of contemplative praying that takes its inspiration from *The Cloud of Unknowing*, authored by a fourteenth-century English Christian. The practice of centering prayer is structured in twenty-minute periods, twice daily, in which we offer to God a simple, loving word or phrase that captures our deepest sense of divine reality. We allow other thoughts, concerns, or conversation to recede. In silence we offer our word as a "dart of love" that yearns in the direction of divine life. Such prayer empties us to receive God's ever-present love. While many choose to exercise this form of prayer in solitude, centering prayer groups offer instruction and supportive community for this formative practice.

Action-Reflection Groups

A fourth model of group formation is the action-reflection group. Inspired by the rich traditions of social justice that have developed in modern Christian denominations, these groups seek to link action on behalf of the world's poor and oppressed persons with life-challenging reflection. The classic instance of such groups is found in the Latin American base community experience. During the middle of the twentieth century, small groups of the most oppressed and impoverished citizens of Latin America began to reclaim the ancient prophetic vision of scripture: God's plea and preference for the "widow and orphan," the dispossessed, the forgotten, the "little ones." These base communities read scripture in light of their own immediate, desperate situation and sought to hear God's liberating word in it. Then they acted out of that word. The group process that gradually developed was a circular one of action (lived experience), followed by reflection (grounded in scripture), which led to new action. When this process is practiced in situations of privilege, such action-reflection groups often focus on acts of service and justice on behalf of marginalized people. Christians involved in peace work; human rights; action to alleviate hunger, discrimination, or housing shortages can in this way ground their activity in profoundly reflective group sharing that is rooted in scripture, social ethics, and prayer.

> *Spirituality is a community enterprise. It is the passage of a people through the solitude and dangers of the desert, as it carves out its own way in the following of Jesus Christ. This spiritual experience is the well from which we must drink.*
>
> —Gustavo Gutiérrez

Group Spiritual Guidance

A final type of formational group is group spiritual guidance. This small community focuses on helping members with ongoing individual discernment. Group guidance may be practiced several ways. In the first, a clearly identified spiritual guide interacts with each member in turn, in the presence of all. Group members are helped to recognize, celebrate, and respond to the Spirit's movement in their lives, as revealed through accounts of their prayer and life experience since last meeting. In the second form of small group guidance, the identified guide's direction of each individual is combined with reflective input from other group members at specified times. In the third form, group members themselves function as spiritual guides for one another.

In this third variation, as developed by the Shalem Institute for Spiritual Guidance,[5] groups are carefully oriented at the institute for the task they are to undertake. Individuals willingly commit themselves to faithful attendance of meetings, discussion with others about their relationship with God, and commitment to the fundamental process. The process is deeply grounded in the practice of shared silence, the art of listening to one another, and in contemplative alertness to the presence of the Spirit. At each meeting one member acts as facilitator, keeping track of time and alerting the group if it moves away from a contemplative mode, tries to "fix" or "rescue," or becomes distracted. After a period of silence, a member shares for ten to fifteen minutes some aspect of his or her journey with God, especially in relation to prayer, since the group last met. If the speaker wishes response from the group, another shared silence is observed, followed by reflection from any who feel led to respond. The process is repeated for each person in the group. Then they pray for absent members and share reflection on their time together. Typical questions for closure might include the following: How is God working here? How did the process go? What do I/we take from this gathering? The fruit of dwelling together in loving intimacy this way is growth in God and compassion for others.

The church is indeed a thriving vineyard with many engrafted branches taking nourishment from Christ, the Vine. But the nurture and cultivation of that vineyard are never solely individualistic. We prune, water, hoe, and fertilize one another's vine gardens as we cultivate our own and as we actively participate with one another in being formed anew.

In group spiritual direction people learn to listen to God's Spirit at work in them for others in the group. As they take the sharing of others into the resting place of shared silence they seek to respond to what has been disclosed out of that prayerful place. Thus there is a collective wisdom available for each person.

—Rose Mary Dougherty

DAILY EXERCISES

Thomas Hawkins writes, "Our selfhood does come to us as a gift. But it is not a gift that God buries deep within us and that we must then individually uncover. It comes to us through those means of grace that God's prevenience has always provided: our often flawed and sometimes destructive relationships with friends, family, and community. . . . Our spiritual journeys require companions."[6]

The scripture passages in these exercises invite us to explore the power of Christ's presence "where two or three are gathered in my name."

EXERCISE 1

Read Mark 6:30-32. These few verses give us a glimpse into the inward/outward rhythm of Jesus' life with the disciples. After having been dispersed for ministry, the disciples gather around Jesus, report and reflect on their actions, and rest with Jesus in a quiet place in preparation for being sent again in ministry.

To what degree does your life reflect this formative rhythm of life in Christ? What relationships or groups help you maintain the Christ-pattern in a purposeful and life-giving way?

EXERCISE 2

Read Matthew 18:15-20. This passage reflects a model by which church members assist one another in working out differences and in seeking to live the peace of Christ. Notice the aspects of the model that you find appealing, challenging, and/or troublesome. Consider why you feel as you do. (With respect to verse 17, keep in mind the extraordinary love with which Jesus treated pagans and tax collectors!)

Turn your attention to members of your church. How do you (or could you) assist one another in facing hurts, forgiving sins, healing wounds, and celebrating the grace of reconciliation in the community? Where do you see situations that cry out for more deliberate application of Christ's reconciling power in community? Hold the situations in prayer with openness to the leading of the Holy Spirit.

EXERCISE 3

Read John 11:1-44. The story of Lazarus illustrates God's resurrection power in Christ to raise the dead to new life. The story climaxes with three requests for the disciples' cooperation: "Take away the stone," "Unbind him," and "Let him go." Reread verses 38-44 while meditating on how the power of Christ can be present among spiritual friends to bear burdens, unbind fetters, and set one another free for new life. Record your insights.

What practices would characterize a mutual commitment to "take away," "unbind," and "let go free"? What parts of you cry out for the liberation such a group could support?

EXERCISE 4

Read Acts 11:25-30; 13:1-3. These and other similar episodes in Acts give us a glimpse of the way Paul, Barnabas, and their fellow missioners related to one another. When they met together, they were not just a support group; they formed a group committed to supporting the Spirit's ministry in and through one another. The practice of listening prayerfully to the Spirit's leading was central to their relationships and their manner of meeting.

Consider your life in the Spirit. With whom do you (or could you) listen to the guidance of the Spirit? Consider the life of your church. How could you be more deliberate about listening together to the guidance of the Spirit for the church's common life and ministry?

Take a few moments now to listen for and to record in your journal the stirring of the Spirit in you regarding the possibilities and power of fuller reliance on the guidance of the Spirit.

EXERCISE 5: DAILY EXAMEN

Use one of the models for daily examen provided for the past two weeks. Or try the approach described below that is based on Jesus' pattern of meeting regularly with his disciples for reflection and rest (see Mark 6:30-32 and Daily Exercise 1 above). Keep your journal at hand for notes.

Gathering. Imagine gathering at week's end in the company of Jesus with Christian friends. Collect yourself in God's presence. Remember and list people and events that gifted your life this week. Write a brief prayer of thanksgiving.

Reporting. Tell Jesus the story of your week as a disciple. What were the high points and low points? Where did you succeed and fail in living your life as a response to God's call? Where were you tested and delivered? Where did you experience God's presence and prompting? Note actions, attitudes, and experiences that were part of your walk. Reflect on patterns and learnings.

Rest. Spend time with Jesus in quiet and in prayer. Allow him to release you from your failures, heal your hurts, and empower you for the challenges ahead. Listen to Jesus as he affirms your life and sends you forth in ministry for the week to come. Record what you see and hear; write what you understand to be your "sending forth" commission.

Remember to review your journal entries for the week in preparation for the group meeting.

Part 5, Week 4

Re-Visioning Our Life As Companions in Christ

Perhaps we have inherited the old prejudice that sees spirituality as essentially a private and interior matter, while our life together in worship and service is public. Nothing could be further from the truth! We can aptly define spirituality as the whole personal process of searching for a vital relationship with God. This process has a profoundly introspective dimension. We must look honestly at ourselves and our present relationship with God, paying attention to the deep hunger for meaning that underscores our lives and listening to the heart's longing. But once we have sensed God's promptings, we must respond. We are called to act, living out our spiritual longings in the wider world, our communities, our workplaces, and our families. The spiritual life is a life of call and response. It involves us utterly and cannot be contained in some isolated inward realm. Spirituality is intensely personal, leading us to appreciate that deep solitude and silence through which God often speaks, but it is never private in the sense that it is "just for me."

It would be wise then to look closely at our corporate life in the church as an environment in which spiritual guidance and discernment can and do take place. In fact, the conviction behind *Companions in Christ* is that the church is a community of grace and spiritual guidance and that the primary task of congregations is to help people enter into and mature in the Christian life. You do not need to be

a pastor or church professional to consider the role of the church in this regard and to see ways that your congregation can respond more fully to people's search for God and fullness of life in Christ. Each of us—whether a member of the church board, choir singer, Sunday school teacher, Bible study participant, youth group volunteer, or participant in weekly worship—is looking to the church for support and guidance in living a life of faithfulness to Christ. But we are more than receivers. We also participate in how the church responds to people's spiritual needs by the way we choose to share and shape our life together in Christ. We are all invited to re-vision our lives as companions in Christ.[1]

Worship as Guidance

When people think about going to church, the first thing they consider is the Sunday worship service. What are we doing when we meet weekly together? What do we expect, envision, and receive? The Sunday service is first and foremost an occasion for shared worship. I think we have become almost oblivious to the deep resonance of that word *worship*. We come together to acknowledge the astonishing and unfathomable mystery that lies at the heart of life itself. We come with our joys, fears, wounds, dreams, and with one another. When we worship, we acknowledge God's presence in our midst.

Our traditions have given us an infinitely rich reservoir of stories, concepts, and symbols through which we can begin to glimpse and appreciate the mystery that is God. We have words, gestures, rituals, and practices that should enable us to worship with great breadth and beauty. They form bridges by which God enters our lives in intimate and transforming ways. We come to hear the Word proclaimed. Proclamation of God's Word does not merely inform us about scripture and Christian ethical demands. We listen to the Word so that we will be transformed, so that it will become the source of our deepest life, so that in it we will "live and move and have our being." We need to come to the Word as the psalmist suggests, like a thirsty doe seeking a stream. Such thirst ought to be foremost in our minds and hearts

The service of worship builds upon our acceptance of God and moves toward forms through which we open ourselves to God's presence. From the music that plays as the service begins, to the times of quiet within the service, a significant function of worship is that of creating space in which people may experience what it means to make space for God.

—Howard Rice

when we hear the Word preached. The Word is a multifaceted, infinitely deep life source. It cannot be reduced to a single interpretation or viewed as a cipher that only trained specialists can decode. The Word proclaimed, heard, seen, and assimilated is the agent of our transformation.

Our shared worship not only draws our attention to the spiritually vital Word; it also invites us into prayer. Prayer! Not rote phrases rattled off but the cry of the human heart aflame with love, the cry of the parched spirit searching for living water. What we bring to worship is our shared aspiration for God. The outflow of our communal breath—our aspiration—that is prayer. We pray when we sing together the hallowed hymns that give our breathing common shape. We pray when we speak the ancient words that Jesus taught us, words that unfold with endless resonance. We pray when we wait in silence together and attend to the shared beating of our hearts. We pray when we greet one another with a kiss of peace, when we allow the wordless carpet of music to usher us into adoration.

Our worship is orchestrated with gestures and rituals, visual and verbal symbols that invite us to enter into the mystery we long for in a heightened way. To be immersed in baptismal waters is to remember and relive the primal energy of birth, of emerging into a new life. To break bread and share a cup together is to enter into a deeply life-sustaining gesture. We become a community of mutual need and mutual nourishment, feeding on divine sustenance by the Spirit, with and for one another.

The sacraments are not rituals we engage in simply out of habit or mere tradition. They are powerful symbolic doors through whose ample generosity we enter a more complete and meaningful experience of who we are—children of God, nourished by the very source of divine life. If we learn to enter into the power of our symbols, worship can become more than a dutiful activity. Our worship can be a primary source of spiritual guidance, allowing God's Word and our words to give new life.

Education and Administration as Guidance

Although worship is primary, there are many other avenues for members of the gathered church to explore their life together in a spiritually vital way. For example, the church educates through worship and preaching, adult and children's Sunday school, Bible studies and youth groups, and its moral and ethical teachings. Spiritually alive education must be intentionally transformational. It is not enough to conceive of the church as a source of fixed answers or a storehouse of information to be dispensed. The church is the bearer of a broad and rich tradition at the heart of which are the Gospels. From generation to generation the church hands on that Gospel-based tradition. However, for tradition to be genuinely alive, each member of the community must appropriate it in a personal, creative way.

Take, for instance, the practice of Bible study. In many churches this has become the preserve of an "authority," perhaps the pastor because of his or her training in biblical scholarship. Yet as you have already discovered, the Word needs to be more than facts and information to take root in our lives. A spiritually nurturing Bible study might include some historical-critical teachings but also fruitfully incorporates the process of prayer and meditation. In a meditative reading of scriptures, persons may engage all their faculties—thinking, feeling, sensation, and intuition. Doing this allows the text to enter them, to interweave with the story of their own lives, to become a prayer, and perhaps to become a question that takes them deeper into the mystery. True education "educes"—it draws forth from the learner her or his capacity for creativity, reflection, and wisdom. In this way, scripture study can become a significant aspect of spiritual guidance in the church.

The church can also exercise spiritual guidance in its administrative functions. Until recently, most churches approached administration more as a business than as a community of spiritual guidance. Congregational boards and committees usually come to meetings with a mind-set to get a job done or solve a problem. How refreshing it has been to learn of churches that are discovering how meetings can be occasions for working in a worshipful way that makes

genuine spiritual discernment possible. Some church leaders now understand committee work and board meetings as times when smaller groups from the larger worshiping community come together to listen prayerfully to God's Word, to one another, and to God's spirit active in their midst. Charles M. Olsen (Presbyterian) and Danny E. Morris (United Methodist), among others, have offered serious attention to "worshipful work" and corporate discernment.[2]

A spiritually alive meeting requires more than opening and closing with prayer. It might, for example, appropriately include time for silence. We have a fine model to observe from the Quakers, who from the start have carried on business meetings as extensions of their silent worship. A meeting opening time also might provide an opportunity for members to share briefly about significant matters in their lives. In part, this sharing helps them release personal agendas early in the meeting and form a caring and compassionate community. Other possibilities include shared prayer and hymn singing, scripture reading, prayerful reflection on where God seems to be moving the group, or open discussions of the spiritual vitality of the church. The idea that church boards, staff meetings, deacons' gatherings, and various committees of the church could provide opportunities for shared discernment is currently quite countercultural. It requires genuine understanding, willingness, and preparation on the part of all involved—but what promise it holds for transforming a congregation's way of life!

Wherever two or three gather in Christ's name, Christ is present. In the midst of conducting business we can have our eyes open to see the Spirit at work through bricks and mortar, dollar signs and newsprint agendas.

—Larry J. Peacock

Outreach and Service as Guidance

Finally, we also can view outreach and service as aspects of spiritual guidance in the church. Action and contemplation are not foes, despite stereotypes to the contrary. In our world, more and more groups dedicated to peace and social justice are considering the deep spiritual resources needed to sustain their action. They are discovering that it is not enough to confront violent structures; they also must cultivate a genuinely nonviolent heart. When church leaders and members reach out to meet the needs of the world, they must not think of it as mere charity—giving money, time, or skills to less fortunate

Spirituality must include what we do as well as how we are, include acts of mercy as much as prayer. . . . To focus all one's spiritual energy inward is to miss meeting Christ in the person of the one who is needy.

—Howard Rice

persons. Such outreach is truly a practice of spiritual formation. Contact with the world's violence and pain; with poor, oppressed, and forgotten persons, is an opportunity for us to be changed. It is a chance to see God's world through a wider lens than our own limited view. Being open to what God has to say through our works of mercy (feeding the hungry, sheltering the homeless, giving drink to the thirsty, clothing the naked, tending the sick, visiting the imprisoned) can be profoundly transforming. Such ministry will challenge and change us. Often we discover that "the poor" are our most important spiritual teachers and guides. Through outreach and service, we can open ourselves to receive spiritual guidance.

A career woman I know once spent a month at a L'Arche community farm. L'Arche is an organization that brings together persons with mental challenges and persons without such challenges into a shared life experience. This woman went with the idea of helping others, fulfilling her Christian duty by using her gifts on behalf of less fortunate persons. Her experience was exactly the reverse. A city girl, she found herself quite helpless on a farm. She had to be constantly tutored in the most gentle and compassionate way by those she had imagined she would serve. As this woman gradually came to accept her dependence on others, she became aware of all the subtle ways she had learned over the years to mask her neediness. Always having to look good was one way. Always having the right answer was another. Always being competent was a third. She came to see that the tables had turned. The very persons she came to help were helping her. They were her spiritual mentors in the way of God's love and the dignity of each human life.

Behind the notion of the church as a genuine community of spiritual guidance is the unsettling idea that we are a people in process, not a people who have "arrived." We are discerners of God's unfolding will, pilgrims on a journey of individual and communal transformation. Whether church professional or layperson, you can begin to envision the role and meaning of church in this light. Every dimension of our life together is a potential spiritual pathway, an avenue through which we are guided by and with one another toward God.

DAILY EXERCISES

Danny Morris and Charles Olsen have written, "Members of the New Testament church believed that God would guide individuals and communities; they expected to be led by the Spirit."[3]

This week's daily exercises invite us to explore scriptures that point to the practice of discernment in the early church and to consider what it would mean to return more fully to this distinctive way of making decisions together in Christ.

EXERCISE 1

Read Exodus 18:1-27. Jethro advises Moses on how to organize the administration of the faith community based on an important principle for ministry and spiritual discernment: "You cannot do it alone." Outline the main points of Jethro's remedy. Where do you see the principles of Jethro's advice in church life? Where do you see the need for any aspect of Jethro's counsel in your congregation or in the way you carry out your calling?

EXERCISE 2

Read Acts 1:12-26. This is the account of the eleven apostles gathered in an upper room to seek a replacement for Judas. We can find in the story several key insights into the practice of discerning God's will in community. What indications do you see of how they prepared their hearts, when they used their heads, where they relied on God, and how they actually sought God's will?

In light of what you find, describe what you see as the necessary condition(s) for discerning God's will as an individual or as a group. Also name your most serious questions or apprehensions about it. Spend your remaining time prayerfully applying your insights to a question or dilemma in your life.

EXERCISE 3

Read Acts 15:1-29. This story shows the Jerusalem church debating and seeking God's will on an issue of enormous volatility and significance for the development of Christianity: whether Gentile converts had to be circumcised according to the law of Moses. Reread the story with an eye toward words and phrases that describe the atmosphere. Record what you see.

Read the story again slowly with an eye toward attitudes, actions, and grace-filled moments that played a role in the story of how the church moves beyond "no small dissension and debate" to a conclusion that "seemed good to the Holy Spirit and to us." Record what you see. What do these insights add to your understanding of how we discern God's will together?

Take a moment to identify a tough issue or question in your church or community. Hold the parties involved in love and prayer.

EXERCISE 4

Read Acts 15:1-29 again. Then look at the list "Some Principles for Discerning God's Will Together" (page 60). Note how you see these principles at work in the story of the Jerusalem church. Look in particular for where you can imagine "shedding" was required in order to move ahead without dividing the community between winners and losers.

Take a moment to remember the tough issue or question you identified yesterday. What would you and others have to lay down and take up in order to move from dissension and debate toward agreement on God's will in the unity of the Spirit? Remember in love and prayer the persons involved.

EXERCISE 5: DAILY EXAMEN

A daily review of life is a way to examine our thoughts, feelings, and experiences in terms of how God is present and how we are responding. It fosters an awareness of God's presence and call in our daily lives. It is also good preparation for the practice of spiritual guidance in any form. This particular model reads as a conversation with God. Keep your journal at hand to make notes.

God, my Creator and Redeemer, I am totally dependent on you. Everything is a gift from you. I give you thanks and praise for the gifts of this day. Give me also an increased awareness of how you are guiding and shaping my life, and of the obstacles I put in your way.

Be near me now and open my eyes as I reflect (in my journal) on:

- Your presence in the events of today:

  _____ ;

- Your presence in the feelings I experienced today:

  _____ ;

- Your call to me:

  _____ ;

- My response to you:

  _____ .

God, I ask for your loving forgiveness and healing. The particular event of this day that I most want healed is

_____ .

The particular gift or grace that I most need is

_____*discipline*_____ .

I entrust myself to your care and place my life in your strong and faithful hands. Amen.[4]

Remember to review your journal entries for the week in preparation for the group meeting.

Some Principles for Discerning God's Will Together

Preparing—Trust and expect that God is with you and will guide you in all matters as they affect the life and ministry that Christ seeks to express in and through us. Prepare yourselves for the guidance of the Spirit by devoting yourselves constantly to prayer.

Framing—Clearly focus the proposition to be tested or the question to be explored.

Grounding—Define the higher, guiding (or missional) principle or criteria to which your considerations must be faithful.

Shedding—Lay down all motives, agenda, and prejudgments that may limit openness to God; become indifferent to all but God's will.

Rooting—Consider texts from the Bible, wisdom from our spiritual heritage, and experiences from our walk with God that illumine the matter.

Listening—Seek out the voices we need to hear and learn from; listen for God's truth in each one.

Exploring—Consider all of the options and paths within the guiding principle.

Improving—Seek to make each option the best it can be rather than amending down those we don't like.

Weighing—Offer the best possible options to God, one at a time, weighing our readiness as a group to accept a proposal.

Closing—Ask all persons present to indicate their level of acceptance of a proposed path. State and register the wisdom that may lie within lingering reservations.

Resting—Allow time for the decision to rest near our hearts in a spirit of prayer. Notice feelings of assurance or anxiousness, peace or heaviness, consolation or desolation.

Adapted from Danny E. Morris and Charles M. Olsen, *Discerning God's Will Together* (Nashville, Tenn.: Upper Room Books, 1997), 66–67.

Part 5, Week 5
Discerning Our Need for Guidance

The longer I live, the more certain I am of one truth (and the less certain I am of many other truths). The one truth is that God can find us only where we are. Contemporary writer Norvene Vest captures this idea wonderfully when she states,

> Whatever my present circumstances, Christ will meet me there. However confused, bewildering, boring, or chaotic my life, God is involved in it right now. No matter how little or how much I think I love and serve God, God is waiting, ready to deepen our relationship.[1]

In other words, a genuine spiritual life can never be forged in some indefinite future when we get it all together, master some spiritual discipline, find more time, get a new job, or finish raising our children. God cannot reach us where we "ought to be"; God can reach us only where we are precisely because we are accepted and loved not for what we accomplish but simply because we have being. Thus we must root any assessment of our need for spiritual guidance in who we really are—in an honest, genuinely humble knowledge of our desires, strengths, weaknesses, and particular life circumstances.

What do we need in the way of companionship at this time and place? As I look back over my life and focus on the period of my late twenties, I see that it was a time of enormous spiritual growth through which I was guided in a variety of ways. The tapestry of those years is rich and complex, but the main outline is as follows: after a period of

God does not wait for us to have our spiritual acts together before reaching out to us and seeking relationship with us. This should be a point of great relief and freedom for us, for while we may strive for a sense of centered-ness and balance, our relationship with God is not dependent upon our success. God's love will remain steadfast regardless.

—Kimberly Dunnam
Reisman

intense upheaval, personal failure, and geographic relocation, I found myself in a religious studies graduate program at a state university. There I met a remarkable professor who had the gift of mentoring students in a manner that went well beyond professional expertise. He was a teacher, and for years after a friend, who sensed the deepest longings of the heart. At the time I was unchurched, yet possessed an aching hunger for God. My professor (who was Lutheran) introduced me to a Franciscan priest at the old Mission Church in town, and the Franciscan gifted me for a long time with a listening ear. Gradually I found myself led into the Roman Catholic communion. There I found a deep structure of liturgy, ritual, history, theology, and spiritual practice that provided the wider spiritual home from which my individual journey could proceed. My university professor, himself engaged in a spiritual quest, also introduced me to a women's community of Cistercian monks with whom I stayed for a period and whose depth of prayer profoundly stamped my spirituality. Through them as well as through my Franciscan guide, parish church, and professor friend, I have continued to meet groups and individuals who have been invaluable companions to me along the way.

Concentric Circles of Guidance

This brief span of several years in my late twenties was eventful and critical. I recall them because they exemplify what Damien Isabell calls the "concentric circles of spiritual direction" in the church.[2]

The outer concentric circle is the "General Spiritual Direction of the Church," the whole structure of worship, music, sacraments, and teachings by which the church directs the attention of her children toward God. In my case, my conversion to a Christian communion allowed me to participate in this general, overarching spiritual direction. The second circle is institutional or "Group Spiritual Direction," groups that enable people to grow in faith and take greater advantage of the richness of the church's general spiritual direction. In my case, the very focused Cistercian women's community provided such a structure. Examples of less tightly knit groups would be organized retreat experiences, Cursillo, Emmaus, support groups, scripture-based groups, covenant groups, and so forth. The third concentric circle of spiritual direction is "One-on-One." My Franciscan priest provided such intentional listening and direction for me during a crucial time. The inmost guidance circle is called "Hidden Directors." Isabell quotes Adrian van Kaam who says, "To find ourselves we need to follow the reactions and responses of fellow human beings to the life directives we are manifesting in our behavior." Guides come to us in many guises, as distant heroes or intimate friends, for a brief season or for the long haul. My graduate professor mentor, who later became my friend, would fall into the category of "hidden directors." The sureness with which he sensed and believed in my emerging best self, long before I did, opened doors to the Spirit-life for me.

This slice of my story is in no way normative for anyone else. It does, however, reveal the variety of overlapping ways in which the church can nurture us into greater intimacy with God. At any specific moment we need to assess: What is God drawing me to at this time? What is the deepest hunger of my heart? How can that hunger be fed? What is feasible, realistic, and appropriate for me, given my particular gifts and limitations and the circumstances in which I find myself?

Our greatest need may be for the church's general spiritual guidance. As Christians, we need to be rooted in church communities that genuinely turn our attention to God. One danger in seeking spiritual community is that we will be forever floating from one "spiritual

high" to another, looking for the perfect faith community that will do it for us. Staying with a church, either a denomination or a congregation, even when things are not going according to our preferences or when conflicts arise, is part of growing in love and faithfulness. We do need the deep wisdom of the church, its rhythms and seasons, Word and table, the gathered community. Our individual journeys, when isolated, can be only as broad and wide as our personal limits. With one another, past and present, we begin to taste the unlimited possibilities in God.

If we are already well rooted in a congregation, we may find our need is for more focused spiritual nurture. Then we may look to one of the three inner circles to deepen our walk with Christ. Although these three are not always discrete categories, distinguishing them is helpful.

Let's begin with the role of hidden directors. Sometimes all we need to draw us closer to God is the listening ear, the shared prayer, or the faithful support of another person. In Christian communities there are often unobtrusive persons graced with wisdom and experience who will share their faith with us. They are not necessarily recognized leaders. Although a pastor, educator (as in my case), or church professional may come into our lives at a critical juncture and point the way, a position of leadership is not essential here. Often an older member of a congregation, ripened in life's challenges, may emerge to walk with us for a time. He or she may listen, console, encourage, and pray for us. Or God may touch us and guide us through a Sunday school teacher, a friend, or a virtual stranger in the faith community. These persons may mold us in surprising ways that we may not recognize until years later. This is the gift of the Christian community and of the Holy Spirit's presence among us.

Some forms of spiritual friendship belong among the "hidden" forms of guidance. Special persons may emerge who give us life. This usually happens quite unexpectedly, perhaps in a social gathering or on an airplane—an experience of utterly surprising grace. A friendship may be fairly fluid, marked by the mutual sharing of the fruits of the Spirit in the context of ordinary work or social contact. Such

Never in the history of the church has it been considered necessary for everyone to have their own "spiritual director." . . . *There is so much in the ordinary Christian life of a good parish or of a good faith-sharing group that is formative. There is so much illumination in life itself.*

—Carolyn Gratton

a relationship can, however, develop into something more intentional, with get-togethers arranged at regular intervals and careful attention paid to equal time for each of the friends to share. Such a person may become a prayer partner.

There are a few questions (cautions) to consider when discerning your need for spiritual companionship. Informal spiritual friendships, while generally rich and as varied as the Spirit's imagining, are not "supervised" in any way. They are often deeply meaningful. But occasionally, the healing, listening ear of a fellow pilgrim can give way to harmful gossip or inappropriate advice. Some people, sensing they have spiritual gifts, take it upon themselves to be judges. I remember hearing of a charismatically gifted woman who went about warning people that she thought she saw the devil at work in their lives. Her meddling left many frightened and confused. As for friendships, they can sometimes mask serious dependencies or become manipulative. Even the healthiest may ignite deep desires that confuse our primary commitments. They can feed an elitist sensibility—"we are the only holy ones in this church"—or create factions. Being rooted in the wider community of faith is an important antidote to any of these possibilities. No guidance relationship should cut itself off from the larger church or produce the sour fruits of judgmentalism, elitism, narrowness, and/or excessive dependency.

Seeking New Forms of Spiritual Guidance

If our longing is for more intentional and formal spiritual guidance, we may wish to seek out a small group or an individual director. One question we might ask ourselves is temperamental or cultural. In the past, have we found ourselves given life primarily in one-on-one settings or in groups? Extroverted persons usually flourish in a group, while more introverted persons often prefer a one-on-one setting. Regardless of our personality profile, are we looking for a spiritual community or an opportunity to dig deeper on issues that might best be dealt with in an individual encounter? Our ethnic or cultural heritage may dispose us toward a group setting rather than one-on-one.

But the two options are by no means mutually exclusive. We may enjoy the ongoing encouragement of a covenant group, while seeing a personal spiritual guide at the same time.

If we find ourselves drawn to seek out a spiritual guide, we need to consider several issues. First, as mentioned earlier, we need to clarify whether we are truly looking for spiritual guidance—support in discerning God's ongoing will. If we want solutions to a specific life problem, then we would probably do better to seek out pastoral counseling, therapy, or a support group. Second, spiritual direction has emerged as a distinct ministry in today's world. Not all pastors or priests make good spiritual directors, and not all spiritual directors are pastors or priests. Seek referrals from church leaders or trusted individuals to find a spiritual guide. Retreat houses, seminaries, and regional or local church offices for spiritual formation can often advise about spiritual guides in a particular region. A spiritual guide or director is ideally accountable to someone else and has some sort of authorization to undertake the ministry. He or she may have been trained in a recognized program, be on the staff of a house of prayer, or be a member of a religious community.

The manual of ethics of Spiritual Directors International (an ecumenical organization concerned with training and supervision in this ministry) states that anyone claiming to provide spiritual direction should be in direction, working with a supervisor, in consultation with a peer group, or have a network of accountability.[3] Furthermore, not all directors are suited to all persons. Feel free to visit with a potential guide, ask questions about expectations and process, and discern whether that person seems a good "fit." Styles of spiritual guidance differ as do the styles of those seeking guidance. As already suggested, consider ethnic, cultural, denominational, and gender distinctiveness when choosing a spiritual guide. The spiritual guide should respect the conscience and individual spiritual path of each person. Although tremendous intimacy and vulnerability may occur in the guidance process, dependency is never the goal. Having a spiritual guide tell you what to do is never conducive to the freedom of the Spirit. One-on-one spiritual direction may or may not be available in your area.

Each soul is unique: no wisdom can simply be applied without discerning the particulars of this life, this situation.

—Eugene H. Peterson

You may have to decide whether a periodic trip out of town to visit a spiritual guide serves your needs or whether a close-to-home, more frequent group experience is more practical. Finally, there is the matter of mutuality in the spiritual guidance relationship. Do you prefer to focus on your issues with another person, or is a mutual model of guidance from peers, as in some group models, more to your taste?

If a group experience draws you, the first step is to ascertain what sorts of groups are already functioning in your congregation or local area. Next, consider what type of group will feed your spiritual hunger. In Week 3 we explored a variety of models—mutual accountability groups, scripture-focused groups, prayer-focused groups, action-reflection groups, and group spiritual direction. Possibly your need may be for a community of support, and many or most of these group models would nurture you. You may find the kind of group that truly draws you is not available in your local area. You might be instrumental in starting such a group.

Next Steps

Perhaps your question is, "What really does draw me?" Sometimes our deeper needs are revealed to us in unexpected ways. A "hidden director" emerges; a hint comes from a friend; a program catches your attention; a painful longing is awakened as you notice an absence in your life. Anything may point the way to what needs to come next.

If you find yourself drawn to begin a group, several factors are essential. Commitment to regular meetings by a small group (three to ten people) is necessary. For many people, a structured program such as Renovaré or *Companions in Christ* can provide at least initial formation and cohesion for a group. Spiritual formation is not just one more experience or thing to learn. It is a process of self- and other-discovery, of change and challenge, of self-transcendence. It occurs within the context of the Word and the transforming spiritual wisdom of the cumulative Christian community. As such, it needs to refer to the sources of Christian tradition. Group spiritual guidance especially underscores our shared life in Christ.

Discerning your need for spiritual guidance requires that you attend to the particulars of your present life. For a single man with a desire to learn more about prayer, commitment to regular, ten-day prayer retreats may be life-giving. A weekly Wednesday "morning with toddlers faith-sharing" (between nursing and diaper changes) may be the joy of a young mother's life. A long-widowed woman who lives alone in a rural farmhouse may find genuine nurture in a faith-sharing group that offers lively exchange and social companionship, while a busy pastor may relish a periodic solitary retreat interspersed with regular visits to a spiritual guide and augmented by a peer prayer circle.

Whatever discernment we make as to our present need for spiritual companionship, we do well to make it with attention to that deep, silent awareness of which we spoke in Week 1. In that awareness is the knowledge that God is alive and working within us, whispering, nudging, hinting, teasing us into a more loving and joyous embrace of God, self, and one another.[4] "For where two or three are gathered in my name, I am there among them" (Matt. 18:20).

DAILY EXERCISES

The author of Hebrews writes, "See to it that no one fails to obtain the grace of God" (12:15). Susanne Johnson, commenting on this and similar biblical mandates, writes, "By its very nature, the church is an ecology of spiritual care and guidance. It is the decisive context for Christian spiritual formation."[5]

This week's daily exercises challenge you to consider your vision for your church and its possibilities as a community of grace and guidance.

As we listen for the steps of God's Spirit in our midst, and as we seek ways to attune our own steps to these, we will find ourselves taking part, not only with God but also with one another, in the healing of the world.

—Frank Rogers Jr.

EXERCISE 1

Read Matthew 5:1-12. The late Clarence Jordan made a good case that the Beatitudes are not blessings pronounced on different kinds of people—the meek, the merciful, the pure in heart, and so on. Rather, they are stages in the experience of only one class of people—the "poor in spirit" who are entering the kingdom and growing as children of God who bear the divine likeness as makers of peace among people.

Meditate on the Beatitudes as a stairway of growth in God's blessing. Identify where you find yourself. What would you have to lay down or take up in order to go to the next step? What kind of companionship or guidance would you need for that to happen? Spend some time listening to what God wants to say to you about these questions.

EXERCISE 2

Read Colossians 1:24–2:7. In this passage, Paul articulates his personal passion and a pastoral goal that motivates all he does: "That we may present everyone mature in Christ." For what do you and your church "toil and struggle"?

Notice phrases and images that illumine what it means to mature in Christ. Rewrite them in your own words. Pay special attention to whether you see the "you" that Paul addresses as individuals, the faith community, or both; and what difference that distinction makes.

EXERCISE 3

Read Hebrews 5:11–6:2. These verses liken some believers to infants who have not yet progressed beyond a diet of milk, even though by now they should be teachers! What kind of spiritual nurture do "milk" and "solid food" consist of? Which is your usual diet?

Imagine your church as a spiritual nutrition center. Design a balanced spiritual diet for persons in your church who want to be "mature" (v. 14). What are the main food groups? Reflect on what it would take for you and other people in the church to represent and provide such a diet. Record your thoughts and feelings.

EXERCISE 4

Read Philippians 1:1-11. Paul begins his epistle by expressing his highest hopes and deepest longings for the church at Philippi. Meditate on Paul's vision and prayer for the people.

Take a few minutes to paraphrase Paul's prayer (vv. 9-11)—or to write a prayer of your own—in a manner that expresses your heartfelt longing "with the compassion of Christ Jesus" for members of your family and faith community. Commit all or part of your prayer to memory. Reflect on what it means to live out your prayer in your family and church.

EXERCISE 5: DAILY EXAMEN

Use a daily/weekly examen provided during a previous week or try this one. The following examen from Marjorie Thompson's book *Soul Feast* is adapted from some examen instructions by Tilden H. Edwards. Keep your journal handy for notes.

> Begin by relaxing your mind. Gently remind yourself of God's presence, and get in touch with your desire to be attentive to that presence during your day. You might offer a simple prayer that the graces of the day will be revealed to your consciousness.
>
> You need not try to find things; simply be "still and open, listening for what might rise from the day." When something surfaces, pay attention to the nature of the grace involved. How was God present? Let yourself feel and express gratitude for the gift.

Then notice how you were present to God or others in the midst of that moment. If you observe that you were unaware of grace, or unresponsive—perhaps holding the reins of ego control—you might breathe a simple prayer like "Lord, have mercy." Let yourself be aware of desire to respond differently another time.

If you observe that you were responsive to, or at least conscious of grace, simply "smile to God with thanksgiving."

Allow something else from your day to rise into awareness; repeat the process. "Thus you are noticing both the hidden presence of God in the day, and your own way of participating in, missing, or resisting that presence."

When you have completed your observations, make note of any responses that seem significant to you. Have you seen something surprising? discovered a pattern in your way of being present to others? received a special sense of grace or gratitude today?[6]

Remember to review your journal entries for the week in preparation for the group meeting.

Materials for Group Meetings

General Rule of Discipleship

To witness to Jesus Christ in the world,
and to follow his teachings through
acts of compassion, justice, worship, and devotion,
under the guidance of the Holy Spirit.

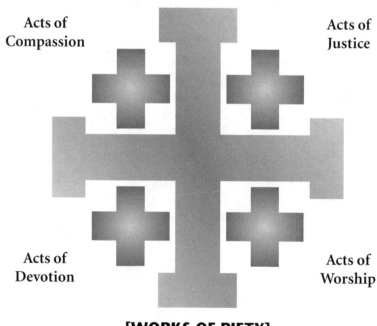

[WORKS OF MERCY]

Acts of
Compassion

Acts of
Justice

Acts of
Devotion

Acts of
Worship

[WORKS OF PIETY]

A GENERAL RULE OF DISCIPLESHIP

"The General Rule is designed to provide faithful disciples with a
simple and straightforward method for Christian living in the world.

For this . . . we need both form and power. Without the power of God's grace, our discipleship becomes a mere formality. Without the form of God's law, our discipleship becomes self-indulgent. Accordingly, the General Rule directs us to follow the teachings of Jesus (form) under the guidance of the Holy Spirit (power)."

Witnessing to Jesus Christ

"Implicit throughout . . . is the cardinal privilege and duty of Christian discipleship: witnessing to Jesus Christ.

Following the Teachings of Jesus

"The next directive is to follow the teachings of Jesus through acts of compassion, justice, worship, and devotion. . . . In these four dimensions of the General Rule, therefore, faithful disciples must not only strive to follow the teachings of Jesus. They must also be ready to hold themselves accountable for doing so."

Under the Guidance of the Holy Spirit

"When we have exercised accountability for all of these works of discipleship, the General Rule directs us to accountability for obedience to the Holy Spirit. . . . Whenever Christian disciples meet together in the name of Christ, they will not only watch over one another in love. Something else will happen. The Spirit of God will be present, working in and through the dynamics of the group, to empower them for service in preparing for the coming reign of God, on earth as in heaven. . . . Identifying these warnings and promptings [of the Holy Spirit] sharpens the discernment of faithful disciples. To go further and to share them with one another means a quantum leap forward in their spiritual life, for their discernment and learnings are thereby greatly multiplied."

All the material on pages 73–74 is reprinted from David Lowes Watson, *Covenant Discipleship: Christian Formation through Mutual Accountability* (Nashville, Tenn.: Discipleship Resources, 1991), 77–94, and is used by permission.

Sample Covenant for a
Covenant Discipleship Group

Knowing that Jesus Christ died for me and that God calls me to be a disciple of Jesus Christ, I desire to practice the following disciplines in order that I might know God's love, forgiveness, guidance, and strength. I desire to make God's will my own and to be obedient to it. I desire to remain in Christ with the help of this covenant so that I might bear fruit for the kingdom of God.

WORSHIP—*I will worship regularly*
- attending Sunday services
- taking communion at least once each month

DEVOTION—*I will take time to meditate and pray each day*
- remembering each member of this group in my prayers
- reading scriptures or passages from a Christian devotional guide each day
- taking time for silent reflection
- paying attention to God's presence, promptings, and warnings in all aspects of my daily life

JUSTICE—*I will seek to be an agent of God's justice and reconciliation in the world*
- upholding human dignity
- speaking out or acting to alleviate injustice wherever I see it
- practicing responsible stewardship of the world's resources in the context of my personal life and community commitments

COMPASSION—*I will practice love for all people*
- including self, family, friends, colleagues
- including my enemies and the strangers I meet

CALL AND RECOMMITMENT—*I will prayerfully plan the best use of my time and resources*
- responding to God's call in the week to come
- balancing time for work, family, friends, and recreation

I make this covenant, trusting in God's grace to work in me, giving me strength to keep it. When I fail in my efforts, I will trust God's grace to forgive me and sustain me.

_____   _____
            Date   Signature

A Covenant Prayer
in the Wesleyan Tradition

I am no longer my own, but thine.

Put me to what thou wilt, rank me with whom thou wilt.

Put me to doing, put me to suffering.

Let me be employed by thee or laid aside for thee,

exalted for thee or brought low by thee.

Let me be full, let me be empty.

Let me have all things, let me have nothing.

I freely and heartily yield all things

to thy pleasure and disposal.

And now, O glorious and blessed God,

Father, Son, and Holy Spirit,

thou art mine, and I am thine. So be it.

And the covenant which I have made on earth,

let it be ratified in heaven. Amen.

From *The United Methodist Hymnal* (Nashville, Tenn.: The United Methodist Publishing House, 1989), 607.

Congregation:
An Ecology of Spiritual Care and Guidance

The concentric circles illustrate how the "church, especially the congregation, is a rich ecology of spiritual care."

"By its very nature, the church is an ecology of spiritual care and guidance. It is the decisive context for Christian spiritual formation. The church offers tacit as well as direct spiritual care and direction as it catches people up in what it is and does."

"The focal setting for spiritual guidance is worship, as we gather to do our liturgy. We initiate, form, and guide Christians through our common prayer and private prayer, through our giving, receiving, rejoicing, confessing, adopting, naming, instructing, washing, anointing, blessing. These are gestures necessary to our formation that the church does *to* us, *for* us, and *with* us."

"Spiritual guidance and care in the congregation must be ongoing and consistent, woven into the fabric of all that happens rather than presented on sporadic occasions as a new program. Many elements of spiritual guidance and care can be initiated and ritualized by pastors and Christian educators who themselves are responsible for breaking the silence about spirituality."

"'See to it that no one fails to obtain the grace of God' (Hebrews 12:15). This charge for ministry and witness is given to the entire company of believers, not simply the clerics. We are to witness to the whole world that the fundamental context of life is the unbounded love and redemptive grace of God."

"To fulfill their vocational call, every Christian already has a spiritual guide in the presence of God's Spirit (1 John 5:7-10). Our task is not to usurp or take over for God, but to help each other pay attention to the motions of grace and the promptings of the Spirit."

"The ultimate context of spiritual formation and guidance, thus, is the environment of grace. *Spiritus creator* is already present, not imported by us, as a creating, converting, guiding presence."

Quotes and diagram on pages 77–78 are taken from Susanne Johnson, *Christian Spiritual Formation in the Church and Classroom* (Nashville, Tenn.: Abingdon Press, 1989), 121–24, 135.

An Annotated Resource List
from Upper Room Ministries®

*T*he following books relate to and expand on the subject matter of this fifth unit of *Companions in Christ*. As you read and share with your small group, you may find some material that particularly challenges or helps you. If you wish to pursue individual reading on your own or if your small group wishes to follow up with additional resources, this list may be useful. The Upper Room is the publisher of all of the books listed, and the number in parentheses is the order number.

1. *Changed from Glory into Glory: Wesleyan Prayer for Transformation* (#9814) by Paul Wesley Chilcote. This book's guidance will assist your first steps in prayer and, if you are experienced in the ways of prayer, you will find resources to deepen your relationship with God in Christ. Attentive prayer, responsive prayer, unceasing prayer, and corporate worship are among topics explored through art, hymns, and reflection.

2. *Under Her Wings: Spiritual Guidance from Women Saints* (#943) by Kathy Bence. *Under Her Wings* offers excerpts from the writings of five women saints and includes scripture readings, the author's meditations, questions for reflection and journaling, and prayer exercises. Through the author's journey and observations you can discover wisdom from the past to illuminate your present.

3. *Discerning God's Will Together: A Spiritual Practice for the Church* (#808) by Danny E. Morris and Charles M. Olsen suggests ways to implement a decision-making approach in church gatherings that is built on prayer and discernment. You were introduced to this basic process in Part 5, Week 4 of *Companions in Christ*. Morris and Olsen believe that church members are weary of the way church business is handled when it does not seem connected with the deeper meanings of their life and faith. This book outlines ten movements in a process designed to help groups seeking to be open to God's will for them. It describes such a process as it might occur in a small group, a congregation, or a church gathering.

4. *Finding a Spiritual Friend: How Friends and Mentors Can Make Your Faith Grow* (#857) by Timothy Jones is an excellent book for persons who want to understand more about the expectations and dynamics of spiritual friendship and ways to strengthen such friendships. The

author writes convincingly that interdependence is at the heart of the faith community. We need one another for strength and guidance as we seek to grow in faithfulness. As an added benefit there are biblical reflections interspersed with the chapters. Although this resource does not contain guidance for small group sessions, the book does provide personal questions for reflection at the end of each chapter.

5. *Discovering Community: A Meditation on Community in Christ* (#870) by Stephen V. Doughty kept a weekly appointment with his journal to answer the question, "Where this past week have I actually seen Christian community?" In his work with over seventy congregations, he found an abundance of times and places where he witnessed genuine community. Out of these experiences, he helps you understand what fosters Christian community and what blocks it. This resource can help to bring a renewed sense of personal calling and commitment to shared ministry for individuals and congregations.

6. *The Pastor as Spiritual Guide* (#846) by Howard Rice positions the specific tasks of pastoral ministry in the larger framework of spiritual guidance. Rice explores preaching, teaching, and administration in the church as opportunities to nurture spiritual growth in members. In developing the image of pastor as spiritual guide, the author examines other prominent images of ministry and shows how these models do not satisfy the full dimensions of leadership. This resource offers a challenging understanding of the role of the congregational leader because it is built on a clear understanding of the mission of the church, namely, the formation of Christian disciples.

Continue your exploration of God's guidance through a study of the Beatitudes by using *Companions in Christ: The Way of Blessedness* with your small group.

The Way of Blessedness
By Marjorie J. Thompson and Stephen D. Bryant
Participant's Book (0-8358-0992-7)
Leader's Guide (0-8358-0994-3)

This nine-week small-group resource explores Jesus' teachings from the Sermon on the Mount commonly referred to as the Beatitudes. The journey invites participants to discover Jesus' vision of the kingdom of God on earth and to develop and live a personal "rule of life" that helps us reside in that kingdom.

Notes

Week 1   How Do I Know God's Will for My Life?

1. Marjorie J. Thompson, *Soul Feast* (Louisville, Ky.: Westminter John Knox Press, 2005), 110–12.
2. Margaret Guenther, *Holy Listening: The Art of Spiritual Direction* (Cambridge: Cowley Publications, 1992), 43.
3. Ben Campbell Johnson, *Invitation to Pray*, rev. ed. (Decatur, Ga.: CTS Press, 1993), 18–22.

Week 2   Spiritual Companions

1. A contemporary exploration of desert spirituality is found in Henri Nouwen's now classic *The Way of the Heart: Desert Spirituality and Contemporary Ministry* (New York: Seabury Press, 1981).
2. *The Wisdom of the Desert*, trans. Thomas Merton (New York: New Directions, 1960), 25–26.
3. *Desert Wisdom*, ed. and illus. Yushi Nomura (Garden City, N.Y.: Doubleday, 1982), 84.
4. Guenther, *Holy Listening*.
5. Howard Rice, *The Pastor As Spiritual Guide* (Nashville, Tenn.: Upper Room Books, 1998), 80–81.
6. Wendy M. Wright, *A Retreat with Francis de Sales, Jane de Chantal and Aelred of Rievaulx: Befriending Each Other in God* (Cincinnati: St. Anthony's Messenger Press, 1996).
7. Tilden H. Edwards, *Spiritual Friend* (New York: Paulist Press, 1980).
8. Howard Rice, *Ministry as Spiritual Guidance* (Louisville, Ky.: Westminster John Knox Press, 1991).
9. Charles M. Olsen, *Transforming Church Boards into Communities of Spiritual Leaders* (Bethesda, Md.: The Alban Institute, 1995). Also Danny E. Morris and Charles M. Olsen, *Discerning God's Will Together* (Nashville, Tenn.: Upper Room Books, 1997).
10. Cf. Esther de Waal, *Living with Contradiction: Reflections on the Rule of St. Benedict* (San Francisco: Harper & Row, 1989).
11. David Lowes Watson, *Covenant Discipleship: Christian Formation through Mutual Accountability* (Nashville, Tenn.: Discipleship Resources, 1994).
12. Kathleen Fischer, *Women at the Well: Feminist Perspectives on Spiritual Direction* (New York: Paulist Press, 1988).
13. Susan Rakoczy, ed., *Common Journey, Different Paths: Spiritual Direction in Cross-Cultural Perspective* (Maryknoll, N.Y.: Orbis Books, 1992).
14. Douglas V. Steere, *Together in Solitude* (New York: Crossroad, 1982), 33–34.

Week 3   Small Groups for Spiritual Guidance

1. Watson, *Covenant Discipleship*.
2. James Bryan Smith, *A Spiritual Formation Workbook* (San Francisco: HarperSanFrancisco, 1993).
3. Vest, *Gathered in the Word: Praying the Scripture in Small Groups* (Nashville, Tenn.: Upper Room Books, 1996).
4. Thomas Keating, *Invitation to Love: The Way of Christian Contemplation* (New York: Continuum, 1994).
5. Rose Mary Dougherty, *Group Spiritual Direction* (New York: Paulist Press, 1995).
6. Thomas R. Hawkins, *Sharing the Search* (Nashville, Tenn.: The Upper Room, 1987), 19, 25.

Notes

Week 4   Re-Visioning Our Life As Companions in Christ

1. A wonderful resource for doing just that is Howard Rice's *The Pastor As Spiritual Guide* (Nashville, Tenn.: Upper Room Books, 1998).
2. See Olsen, *Transforming Church Boards*, and Morris and Olsen, *Discerning God's Will Together*.
3. Morris and Olsen, *Discerning God's Will Together*, 25.
4. Adapted from *Forgiveness: A Guide for Prayer* by Jacqueline Bergan and S. Marie Schwan (Winona, Minn.: St. Mary's Press, 1985), 7-8. Used by permission of S. Marie Schwan.

Week 5   Discerning Our Need for Guidance

1. Norvene Vest, *No Moment Too Small: Rhythms of Silence, Prayer, and Holy Reading* (Kalamazoo, Mich.: Cistercian Publications, 1994), 6.
2. Damien Isabell, *The Spiritual Director: A Practical Guide* (Chicago: Franciscan Herald Press, 1976).
3. Spiritual Directors International, www.sdiworld.org.
4. A helpful resource in discernment is *A Guide to Spiritual Discernment*, comp. Rueben Job (Nashville, Tenn.: Upper Room Books, 1996).
5. Susanne Johnson, *Christian Spiritual Formation in the Church and Classroom* (Nashville, Tenn.: Abingdon Press, 1989), 121.
6. Marjorie J. Thompson, *Soul Feast*; adapted from Tilden H. Edwards, *Living in the Presence: Disciplines for the Spiritual Heart* (San Francisco: Harper & Row, 1987), 84.

Sources and Authors
of Margin Quotations

Week 1   How Do I Know God's Will for My Life?

Suzanne G. Farnham et al., *Listening Hearts: Discerning Call in Community* (Harrisburg, Pa.: Morehouse, 1991), 14.

Danny E. Morris and Charles M. Olsen, *Discerning God's Will Together* (Nashville, Tenn.: Upper Room Books, 1997), 16.

Jeannette A. Bakke, *Holy Invitations: Exploring Spiritual Direction* (Grand Rapids, Mich.: Baker Books, 2000), 223.

William A. Barry and William J. Connolly, *The Practice of Spiritual Direction* (New York: The Seabury Press, 1982), 8.

Thomas R. Hawkins, *A Life That Becomes the Gospel* (Nashville, Tenn.: Upper Room Books, 1992), 36.

Week 2   Spiritual Companions

William A. Barry, *Spiritual Direction and the Encounter with God* (New York: Paulist Press, 1992), 92.

Kenneth Leech, *Soul Friend* (San Francisco: Harper & Row, 1977), 37.

Larry J. Peacock, *Heart and Soul* (Nashville, Tenn.: Upper Room Books, 1992), 24.

Morris and Olsen, *Discerning God's Will Together*, 39–40.

Week 3   Small Groups for Spiritual Guidance

Tilden H. Edwards, *Spiritual Friend* (New York: Paulist Press, 1980), 96.

Peacock, *Heart and Soul*, 26.

Gustavo Gutiérrez, *We Drink from Our Own Wells* (Maryknoll, N.Y.: Orbis Books, 1984), 137.

Rose Mary Dougherty, *Group Spiritual Direction: Community for Discernment* (New York: Paulist Press, 1995), 36.

Week 4   Re-Visioning Our Life As Companions in Christ

Howard Rice, *The Pastor As Spiritual Guide* (Nashville, Tenn.: Upper Room Books, 1998), 97.

Peacock, *Heart and Soul*, 12.

Rice, *The Pastor As Spiritual Guide*, 132.

Week 5   Discerning Our Need for Guidance

Kimberly Dunnam Reisman, *The Christ-Centered Woman* (Nashville, Tenn.: Upper Room Books, 2000), 18.

Carolyn Gratton, *The Art of Spiritual Guidance: A Contemporary Approach to Growing in the Spirit* (New York: Crossroad, 1993), 107.

Eugene H. Peterson, *Working the Angles* (Grand Rapids, Mich.: William B. Eerdmans, 1987), 104.

Frank Rogers Jr., "Discernment" from *Practicing Our Faith*, ed. Dorothy C. Bass (San Francisco: Jossey-Bass Publishers, 1997), 118.

COMPANION SONG
Piano Accompaniment Score

Lyrics by Marjorie Thompson

Music by Dean McIntyre

Optional cut for short version: omit measures 19-34.

Companions in Christ
Part 5 Author

Wendy M. Wright holds the John F. Kenefick Chair in the Humanities at Creighton University in Omaha, Nebraska. A noted writer in the field of contemporary spirituality, her articles can be found in *Weavings®* and other leading journals of the spiritual life. She has published several books, including a trilogy on the seasons of the Christian year for Upper Room Books: *The Rising, The Vigil*, and *The Time Between*.

Journal